STRANGERS ON A TRAIN

Arsenal Pulp Press | Vancouver

STRANGERS ON A TRAIN

A Queer Film Classic

Jonathan Goldberg

STRANGERS ON A TRAIN: A Queer Film Classic
Copyright © 2012 by Jonathan Goldberg

ARSENAL PULP PRESS
Suite 101 – 211 East Georgia St.
Vancouver, BC V6A 1Z6
Canada
arsenalpulp.com

Efforts have been made to locate copyright holders of source material wherever possible. The publisher welcomes hearing from any copyright holders of material used in this book who have not been contacted.

Queer Film Classics editors: Matthew Hays and Thomas Waugh

Cover design by Shyla Seller
Text design by Gerilee McBride
Edited for the press by Susan Safyan
Author photograph by Michael Moon

Printed and bound in Canada

LIBRARY AND ARCHIVES CANADA CATALOGUING IN PUBLICATION

Goldberg, Jonathan
	Strangers on a train / Jonathan Goldberg.

(A queer film classic)
Includes bibliographical references, filmography, and index.
Issued also in electronic format.
ISBN 978-1-55152-482-5

	1. Strangers on a train (Motion picture). 2. Homosexuality in motion pictures. 3. Strangers in motion pictures. I. Title. II. Series: Queer film classics

PN1997.S77G64 2012   791.43'72   C2012-905839-4

FSC
www.fsc.org
MIX
Paper from responsible sources
FSC® C103214

CONTENTS

ACKNOWLEDGMENTS

Thanks to Jonathon Auxier and his colleagues at the Warner Bros. Archive for making research there a pleasure; to Jenny Romero at the Margaret Herrick Library for alerting me to production code documents there and supplying me with copies; to Thomas Waugh and Matthew Hays, for including me in the Queer Film Classics series, and to everyone at Arsenal Pulp who helped along the way, with special thanks to Shyla Seller for turning a lobby card into a striking cover image, and to Susan Safyan for her superb copyediting. To Marcie Frank, for a reassuring reading of the manuscript in its final form; to J. Hal Rogers for some good brainstorming, helpful on more than one front; to Brent Dawson, remarkable in so many ways, for guiding me through strange technologies; and to Michael Moon, for being there all the along the way. I record with pleasure the numerous students at Johns Hopkins and Emory with whom I have discussed Hitchcock, Highsmith, and queer theory. Were I to make a list of them, Zachary Samalin would be at the top.

SYNOPSIS

Strangers Bruno Antony (Robert Walker) and Guy Haines (Farley Granger) meet on a train leaving Washington, DC's Union Station. Guy is heading to Metcalf, his hometown, to arrange a divorce from his wife Miriam (Laura Elliott) so that he can marry Anne Morton (Ruth Roman), a US senator's daughter. Bruno recognizes Guy as a tennis star and as someone he has seen in the society columns linked to Anne Morton. Bruno quickly deduces Guy's marital difficulties, and after telling Guy about his own hatred of his father, he proposes they solve their problems by swapping murders, committing undetectable, motiveless crimes. Guy apparently entertains Bruno's idea; exiting his compartment, he leaves behind the cigarette lighter Anne had given him, engraved "A to G."

Guy meets with Miriam, but fails to get her to agree to a divorce. He calls Anne to let her know; above the roar of a passing train, he shouts that he would like to strangle Miriam. During a phone call to Guy, Bruno discovers that Miriam has refused to grant Guy a divorce. He proceeds to Metcalf; finding Miriam's address in a phonebook in the same booth from which Guy had called Anne, he follows Miriam to a fairground where he strangles her, pocketing her eyeglasses before he leaves. These he presents to Guy, who has just returned home to his Washington, DC, apartment. Bruno convinces Guy not to go to the police since they would be bound to suspect him as the one who had a motive for the crime. Guy goes to Senator Morton's home, where the senator (Leo G. Carroll) and his daughters Anne and Barbara (Patricia Hitchcock) already know about Miriam's murder, and that the Metcalf police want to speak to him. Guy returns to Metcalf, only to discover that drunken Professor Collins (John Brown), whom he met on the train, cannot provide an alibi for him, since he has no memory of their meeting. Hennessey (Robert Gist) and Hammond (John Doucette), two policemen, are assigned to tail Guy.

Bruno's repeated frustrated attempts by phone and letter to contact Guy and get him to go through with their bargain incite him to come out into the open; at the Mellon Gallery, Anne regards Bruno with suspicion when he accosts Guy. At a tennis club, Bruno watches Guy play a game and finds himself mesmerized by Barbara's resemblance to Miriam (both brunettes wear glasses); and later, at a party at Senator Morton's, Bruno almost strangles Mrs Cunningham (Norma Varden), a guest, while staring at Barbara. Anne guesses that Guy had Bruno kill Miriam; he tells her what happened. Guy calls Bruno, claiming he will go through with their bargain. Evading the police, he arrives at the Antony house only to find Bruno in his father's bed; when he tells Bruno he will not go through with the plan, Bruno promises revenge. Anne attempts to get Bruno's mother (Marion Lorne) to intervene, but finds her too addled to assist. Bruno intimates to Anne that he plans to leave the lighter at the fairground where he strangled Miriam, thus incriminating Guy.

In a final sequence, Bruno goes to Metcalf while Guy must play a tense tennis match in Forest Hills before he can try to stop Bruno. Bruno accidentally drops the lighter down a sewer drain soon after alighting in Metcalf; his struggles to regain it are cross cut with Guy's tennis match. Finally, Guy wins, catches a train to Metcalf, and heads to the amusement park where the two confront each other on a merry-go-round. The police attempt to shoot Guy, but instead kill the merry-go-round attendant. Guy and Bruno fight as the merry-go-round whirls out of control; Bruno is crushed when it is stopped. Only as Bruno dies does he open his hand, revealing the lighter he had intended to plant. Guy calls Anne to say all is okay; in the last shot of the film, they are on a train together when a stranger accosts him, recognizing him. He and Anne hurry away.

CREDITS

Strangers on a Train, 1951, USA, English, 100–101 minutes,
black and white, RCA Sound System, 1.37 : 1
Warner Bros. Pictures, Inc.
Director and Producer: Alfred Hitchcock
Based on the Patricia Highsmith novel *Strangers on a Train*
Adaptation: Whitfield Cook
Screenplay: Raymond Chandler and Czenzi Ormonde

Principal Cast:
Farley Granger (Guy Haines)
Ruth Roman (Anne Morton)
Robert Walker (Bruno Antony)
Leo G. Carroll (Senator Morton)
Patricia Hitchcock (Barbara Morton)
Laura Elliott (Miriam Haines)
Marion Lorne (Mrs Antony)
Jonathan Hale (Mr Antony)
Howard St. John (Captain Turley)
John Brown (Professor Collins)
Norma Varden (Mrs Cunningham)
Robert Gist (Hennessey)
John Doucette (Hammond)
Howard Washington (waiter)

Crew:
Production Associate: Barbara Keon
Director of Photography: Robert Burks
Original Music: Dimitri Tiomkin
Music Director: Ray Heindorf
Sound: Dolph Thomas
Art Director: Ted Haworth
Set Decorations: George James Hopkins
Wardrobe: Leah Rhodes
Special Effects: H.F. Koenekamp
Makeup Artist: Gordon Bau

Filmed in Los Angeles and on location in New York City,
Washington, DC, Danbury and Darien, CT.
Produced October–December 1950; Released June 30,
1951.

DVD with original Hollywood and so-called British
version, WB 15324.
Two-disc special edition with commentaries, and final
release and preview versions, WB 31975.
Lux Radio Theater adaptations, 1951 and 1954, AUK CD
0041.

Robert Burks nominated for an Academy Award for Best
Cinematography.

ONE: PRODUCTION NOTES AND THE MAKING OF A QUEER FILM CLASSIC

Strangers on a Train (1951) is not the only film by Alfred Hitchcock that might be termed a queer classic. Lee Edelman offers bravura chapters on *North by Northwest* (1959) and *The Birds* (1963) in *No Future: Queer Theory and the Death Drive*, for example. These are not the only instances of queer readings of Hitchcock, of course, although they are particularly inspiring ones for me in this study. Even Camille Paglia's BFI monograph on *The Birds*, although certainly not written under the auspices of queer theory—indeed, quite resistant to theory of most any kind—comes into its orbit when her delight in the film, and especially her admiration for Tippi Hedren, leads Paglia to claim for herself a viewing position that she ascribes to "gay men and drag queens" (1998, 44).

Versions of such queer cross-identification also mark the genesis of *Strangers on a Train*. Hitchcock's film takes its cue from the 1950 novel with the same title by Patricia Highsmith. This was Highsmith's first novel; in 1950, she was an unknown writer just shy of thirty years old. Hitchcock was prescient in his discovery of her *Strangers on a Train*, and it gave him a good deal more than a title. Hitchcock's responsiveness to this dark and disturbing work marks my point of contact with his film. I came to it from my attachment to Highsmith, and came to Highsmith in large measure thanks to her depictions of intense male-male relationships. Other well-known film directors after Hitchcock have found Highsmith's novels irresistible, especially those in which Tom Ripley is the central character.[1] Highsmith, a lesbian writer who infrequently represented lesbians, is best known for these novels; indeed, she identified with Ripley, sometimes even signing herself "Tom." Tom can be regarded as pathological (he kills people to get what he wants), and his supposed pathology can be coupled with his elusive sexuality. His desire to have what other men have is easily understood as his desire to have other men; however, from the second novel on, he is married, and perversely, happily so. Tom is no poster boy for gay identity— or for any identity easy to label. For me, that's part of his charm. The questions about sexuality and pathology he raises are anticipated by Charles Anthony Bruno in Highsmith's first novel; this is the character who provides the template for Hitchcock's Bruno Antony. Understanding him has been central to much critical discussion of sexuality in the film, the topic I pursue in the second chapter of this study: finding terms for what ties him to Guy Haines provides me with the opportunity to think about male-male relationships beyond normative parameters. I pursue further the connections

---

1. *Plein Soleil* (René Clément, 1960) is the first film based on *The Talented Mr. Ripley*. Anthony Minghella's 1999 film with the same title is the most recent. Films based on subsequent Ripley novels begin with *Der amerikanische freund* (Wim Wenders, 1977) and include Liliana Cavani's *Ripley's Game* (2004). Claude Chabrol's *Le cri du hibou* (1987) is also based on a Highsmith novel, although not one with Ripley in it.

16

between Hitchcock's film and Highsmith's novel in the third chapter: Highsmith's novel—in which Guy goes through with the murder plot initiated on the train—can appear as far more radical than Hitchcock's film insofar as it suggests how socially alienated the protagonists are from acceptable forms of behavior. However, I've come to value Hitchcock's film precisely for the ways in which its apparent distinction between Guy and Bruno houses insidious suggestions of identification between them that are perhaps even more provoking than Highsmith's outrages.

It is a particularly nice coincidence that Hitchcock himself was on a train when he first encountered Highsmith's novel. He was returning to the West Coast after East Coast screenings of *Stage Fright* (1950) and had with him the galleys of her book, which was published in mid-March. Hitchcock is reported to have negotiated movie rights anonymously with Highsmith, according to John Russell Taylor, initially offering her $2,000 (1978, 213), although Joan Schenkar more plausibly suggests that Margot Johnson, Highsmith's agent, did the negotiating (2009, 572). When, by April 20, they had concluded their discussions (according to a May 25 letter from R. J. Obringer in the legal department at Warner Bros.), the figure had risen to $7,500. This is the amount stipulated on the May

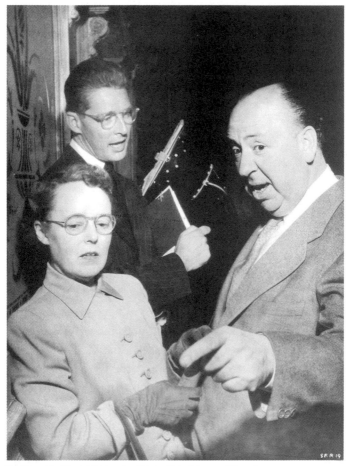

FIGURE 1. The Three Hitchcocks. Warner Bros. Pictures / Photofest.

19 contract signed by Hitchcock and by Highsmith, who styled herself there as "Mary Patricia."

Hitchcock was not alone on a train when he first read *Strangers on a Train*. With him were his wife Alma Reville and Whitfield Cook, the screenwriter for *Stage Fright*. Cook was a family friend and had been one for several years—the relationship started after he had directed the Hitchcocks' daughter Patricia in a stage version of his novel *Violet* in 1946. Indeed, by early 1950, he was so much an intimate that Patrick McGilligan, recounting their train trip together, refers to Cook, Hitchcock, and Reville as "the three Hitchcocks" (2003, 441). Cook and Reville had worked together on Hitchcock scripts and, as McGilligan puts it, "Alma's affection for Cook spilled into passion." Did Hitchcock know that he was one of "three Hitchcocks"? Did he realize that he was in a ménage à trois? McGilligan supposes that he did not; that it would not have occurred to Hitchcock because he assumed that Cook, a bachelor, was gay and therefore "safe" as Reville's constant companion.

The "three Hitchcocks" is a queer configuration. According to McGilligan, Cook and Reville began an affair in 1948 that lasted at least a year or two. During these years, Cook was often involved in writing movie scripts, frequently collaborating with the Hitchcocks. That is, in fact, why he and Hitchcock were reading the galleys of Highsmith's forthcoming novel. Cook went on to write the initial treatment of the novel. He was the right person for the job, McGilligan opines, especially when it came to making what McGilligan assumes to be Bruno's homosexuality a "subtext of the film": "Whitfield Cook knew how to code the signals from his circle of friends, and in his hands the film's Bruno became a dandy, a mama's boy who speaks French, and who professes ignorance of women" (2003, 442). McGilligan's remark appears to share Hitchcock's supposition about Cook's sexuality, even though he insists at the same time that Cook was Reville's lover and that Hitchcock was wrong to assume that Cook was gay.

This fascinating triangle of the "three Hitchcocks" provides a convenient frame for posing the kinds of questions of identity and identification, questions of knowledge, that Eve Kosofsky Sedgwick's *Epistemology of the Closet* taught us to see as crucial to any queer inquiry. They bear on how we come to understand Guy and Bruno, I would venture. When we add to the queer triangle the fourth figure of the critic (in this instance McGilligan, with his unreconciled double views about Cook's sexuality and Hitchcock's suppositions), we can locate the kinds of questions I will raise as we continue. How does one—should one—attempt to determine questions of sexuality—who is, who isn't, on screen, in real life? Who knows what about whom and upon what basis?

Scripts
The route from Hitchcock's initial encounter with *Strangers on a Train* to the final script of the film was not all that straightforward. The film takes from the novel

pretty directly the meeting of Bruno and Guy on the train and Bruno's murder of Guy's wife as part of the proposed bargain of the exchange of murders. As I've noted, Guy does kill Bruno's father in the novel, whereas in the film he does not go through with Bruno's plan. In the film, Bruno transfers his fascination with Miriam to Barbara, a character who has no equivalent in the novel. Bruno's attempt to plant Guy's cigarette lighter also is not in the novel, nor the tennis match, nor the final return to the scene of the crime. In the novel, Guy is not a tennis pro. Bruno dies before the novel ends, and it is Guy who is apprehended as a murderer. These changes to the plot of Highsmith's novel are all in Cook's treatment. In reviewing it and the subsequent treatment and scripts by Raymond Chandler—the latter ultimately rejected for a final script provided by Czenzi Ormonde, a Warner Bros. employee—I want to highlight the ways in which these films scripts begin to provide the matrix of sexuality that ultimately made Hitchcock's film a queer classic. These scripts wrestle with entrancing questions of sexual identity and sexual identification.

The copy of Whitfield Cook's treatment of *Strangers on a Train* in the Warner Bros. Archives is dated June 20, 1950; although only Cook's name appears on the title page, it's safe to assume that Hitchcock played a part in it, in that

FIGURE 2. "Is your name Miriam?" Barbara's face, Bruno's thought. DVD still.

discussions they had on the train and subsequently lie behind much of Cook's text. Many of the most memorable visual effects of the film are already to be found in this initial treatment: Bruno's tie clip with his name on it; shadowy Bruno following Miriam and her companions to the island in the amusement park; the reflection of Miriam's murder in her eyeglasses; the lone "solitary diminutive" (32a) figure of Bruno before the Jefferson Memorial; Bruno's unmoving head at the tennis game; the evocation of the whirling merry-go-round and the calliope the first time Bruno sees bespectacled Barbara and again at the Senator's party; the cross-cutting of Guy's Forest Hills tennis match and Bruno's return to Metcalf to plant the lighter, which here, as in the film, he loses down a drain; the final fight on the out-of-control whirligig. A number of the most memorable lines of the film can also be found in this first treatment. The initial encounter on the train, for example, has Guy responding to Bruno's claim to be a bum—or so he says his father thinks—with a demurral and a response—"I don't think you know *what* you want" (3). The affect in this response is noted not just in the under-lining (it survives in Farley Granger's delivery of the line) but also in the written direction that indicates that Guy is to say the line with a smile.

In this version of the initial encounter on the train, there is no mention of a Senator's daughter, just an irritating wife who needs to be disposed of. The fact that Guy is not intent on a new marriage makes the encounter a bit easier to imag-ine as a scene of potential seduction. Nonetheless, Guy does not go any further in terms of reciprocating Bruno's advances in Cook's treatment than he does in the film; he rebuffs his notion that the way to establish their relationship is to mur-der for each other.

The version of the Antony family offered in the treatment supports the possibility that we can understand the initial scene as an attempted pickup by suggesting the kind of unsa-vory family situation that 1950s psychology assumed could produce a gay man. Bruno's father is depicted as a brute;

his mother, a former chorus girl, sports a black eye that he's given her. Moreover, his father knows that his son would like to kill him and is quite sure he could never do it: he taunts Bruno as a "mother's boy" (16). What this adds up to is more or less spelled out in a June 30, 1950 Warner Bros. internal memo by one G.M.S., who viewed the film in light of the Motion Picture Association Production Code (the memo is archived in the Margaret Herrick Library Production Code Administration file). Picking up on this depiction of Bruno as a "mother's boy" and his desire to murder his father, G.M.S. worries about the "objectionable flavor" of this family scene: "As outlined in the treatment, this relationship...seems to infer a perverted attitude."

These suggestions of perversity, of Bruno's effeminacy and passivity, are highlighted a scene later in Cook's treatment. When Bruno arrives in Metcalf to murder Miriam, he seeks her at the dress shop that she runs, in this version of the story. Staring into the window, "his reflection takes its place among the actual models of women in their various stylized postures" (18).

Later, furthering this effeminate characterization, when Bruno presents Guy with Miriam's glasses, he crumples in the face of Guy's outrage and attempts to soothe him. Having initially threatened to plant Guy's lighter on the scene in order to incriminate him, he returns the lighter to him in his attempt to continue to ingratiate himself with Guy. (This act of friendship with Guy necessitates an awkward moment

FIGURE 3. Wonderful to kill for love. DVD still.

later when Bruno has to steal the lighter in order to plant it.)
It is in the context of concern for and commiseration with
Guy that Bruno utters a version of the lines that survive in
the film: "You must be tired, Guy, after that long trip. I know
I am. I've sure had a strenuous evening" (25). One can almost
hear Robert Walker's insinuating, feline voice. After this conversation with Guy, Bruno keeps popping up, phoning, leaving notes—more often than he does in the film, less so than
in the novel where his uncanny ability to materialize points to
his role as Guy's double. Anne's suspicions about Bruno's role
in the murder of Miriam finally are articulated—as they will

be in the film—after Bruno has all but strangled one of the Senator's guests. It is then that she voices her belief that Guy had Bruno murder Miriam. However, here there is a queer twist in Cook's treatment: Anne wishes Guy had done it himself, rather than leaving it to Bruno. Anne sees Guy as passive and wishes he were more assertive; she has her doubts about Bruno and about Guy's relationship to him. In a word: Anne suspects their "perverted" relationship.[2]

That suspicion seems part and parcel of Cook's treatment. His Bruno and Guy are alike: both are presented as passive. Bruno proves his manliness by murdering a woman and by attempting to dominate Guy. Anne admires such manliness. So too does her younger sister Barbara, who voices her appreciation (as she will in the film) for men who kill for love, an appreciation that (unknowingly) has Bruno as its object. Barbara is represented as something of an intellectual: that's why she wears glasses. Only seventeen, she is reading the Kinsey report on women. There is certainly something a bit perverse about her, too.

Cook's treatment opens with a description of an unidentified man on a train—Bruno, presumably—killing a fly. This classic pathological behavior finds its echo in the final scene of the treatment in which Bruno blurts out his guilt in the

---

2. These suspicions linger in the stage direction in an October 18 version of the screenplay, which describes Anne at the country club this way: "She is looking at Bruno, wondering what mystery lies behind this strange individual and why he and Guy have disclaimed any previous acquaintance" (79).

police station as he compulsively repeats his notions about everyone wanting to commit murder. Much as Bruno blames Guy in this outburst for not going through with the plan, he blames himself more for choosing Guy. In Cook's treatment, there are broad hints that Bruno's pathology resides in his sexuality. Pathological is also the summary judgment about Bruno that Hitchcock made in his conversation with Truffaut: "As for Bruno, he's clearly a psychopath" (1983, 199).

Given the likelihood that Cook's treatment represents Hitchcock's plans, it's no surprise how much it anticipates the film. Nonetheless, it does so more than might have been expected thanks to the subsequent complicated and unhappy history of the script. As he usually did, Hitchcock proceeded by turning Cook's initial treatment over to someone else to provide dialogue and a full-scale screenplay. What happened this time has been told by any number of Hitchcock biographers; their source, predictably, is Hitchcock himself. In an interview with Charles Thomas Samuels, for example, Hitchcock said: "I had terrible trouble getting my treatment dialogued. Eight writers turned me down. They couldn't visualize the story" (Gottlieb 2003, 149). Raymond Chandler, the writer finally chosen, was Hitchcock's ninth choice, in this account. A memorandum in the Warner Bros. Archives dated July 7 indicates that Chandler was employed at $2,250 per week with a five-week minimum guaranteed. This was, Chandler remarked in a letter, "very high for present conditions in Hollywood" (MacShane 1981, 223). Since this deal was struck only two weeks after Cook completed his treatment, I wonder whether Hitchcock was exaggerating his difficulty in finding a screenwriter. Perhaps only after the choice of Chandler proved unfortunate, Hitchcock wanted him to seem like anything but his first choice. Donald Spoto, following the lead provided by Hitchcock, reports that Chandler had difficulties with Hitchcock's "visual requirements" (1983, 322); Bill Krohn echoes him, claiming that "Chandler had trouble thinking visually" (2000, 116). Visualizing was not the only problem, however.

Chandler's correspondence is filled with complaints about Hitchcock, and it is certainly the case that much that Chandler wrote did not find its way into the film. Chandler produced a revised treatment dated July 28 and a first draft of a screenplay by August 25. A month later a memo dated September 25 indicates that Czenzi Ormonde had been employed to revise the script. She was paid $500 a week, and a November 13 memo indicates that her work had been completed by November 11. Ormonde is usually given full credit for the final script; it would appear that her job was to restore Cook and Hitchcock's original conception and largely to erase Chandler's work. Nonetheless, Chandler's name does appear in the film's credits, although he had thought of removing

FIGURES 4 and 5. Feet walking. DVD stills.

it. The decision to keep it there could have been a cour-
tesy extended by the studio; most likely, both Warner Bros.
and Chandler capitalized on the cachet of having his name
attached to Hitchcock's film. But I'd venture to say there is a
bit more to the story. While Ormonde's final script is often
far from Chandler's, she did not abandon it completely. Nor
is the final version simply hers. For one thing, it certainly represents Hitchcock's desires for the film. Whereas his role in
Cook's initial treatment can only be surmised, as early as the
September 30 temporary script, which lacks any authorial
attribution, "Hitchcock and Keon" are penciled in on the title
page; screenplays produced from October 21 to November
23 with Ormonde's name on them have in parentheses below
"with revisions by Alfred Hitchcock and Barbara Keon"
(Keon was Ormonde's boss at Warner Bros.).

Chandler had insisted on working alone rather than at the
studio and complained alternatively about Hitchcock's inter-
ference and his neglect. Part of the story as to why Chandler

was fired is that he failed to work alongside Hitchcock. There is anecdotal evidence of arguments with Hitchcock as well as of Chandler's out-of-control alcoholic behavior. Despite his claimed lack of visual acuity, however, Chandler has to be credited for one of the strongest visual effects of the film, the initial sequence as Guy and Bruno make their way through the train station for their fated and accidental meeting. "The story begins with feet walking" is the opening sentence of Chandler's July 28, 1950 revised treatment. Chandler's screenplay keeps this opening, remaining close to the stunning initial sequence of the film.

Of course, it is entirely possible that the opening sequence was Hitchcock's idea, as he seems to claim in his discussion with Truffaut (1983, 195). Not merely consequential for the film, this visual figure of feet walking suggests what I take to be a crucial point—how alike, how minimally different, Bruno and Guy are, the difference between sports shoes and more conservative brogues. Moreover, it's the athlete Guy who wears the business shoes, and Bruno who wears the black-and-white sports shoes. How much can you tell about someone from the shoes they wear, especially when that's all you see? The two men are at first faceless, withholding thereby the part of the human anatomy that supposedly delivers the site on which character difference is registered. The two men are linked below the waist.

In Chandler's initial treatment, the similarity between Guy and Bruno is spelled out more explicitly than it is in Cook's.

There are strong suggestions that Bruno's behavior is to be attributed to his supposed homosexuality. As in Cook, this requires a maternal fixation; in Chandler's treatment, Bruno still has a glamorous mother to whom he is devoted. "She looks a cool and fascinating thirty, at most," he writes (16). When Bruno parts from his mother to go to Metcalf to murder Miriam, he tells her that he has a date; his mother coos with pleasure since, she says, Bruno does not usually seem interested in girls. With heavy-handed irony, Bruno tells her how "special" this girl is. If he can't have his mother, it seems, he wants no other woman. He wants Guy, and to have him he needs to release him from his mistaken mate. (In Chandler's treatment, however, Bruno knows from the start that Guy has a new woman in view; however, Bruno opines here, as he does in the film, that Anne is more a career opportunity than a love interest.) Later, after Bruno has murdered Miriam, and after a series of scenes in which he stalks Guy and Anne, Bruno talks to Guy on the phone, and complains that Guy is avoiding him: "I like you. Why can't we get together…I want to be your friend" (52). This sounds like the Bruno of Highsmith's novel, but the next bit of Chandler's script does not: Bruno sends a messenger boy to Guy, but not before making a pass. "It is obvious to any sophisticated person what the messenger boy thinks Guy is," (60) Chandler's treatment reads. This slip of the pen—Chandler writes "Guy" when he means "Bruno"—is telling. By writing "Guy" when he means "Bruno," Chandler suggests that Guy as easily as Bruno might try to pick up a boy. Any "sophisticated person," it seems, will realize that both men are gay.

In his treatment, Chandler delivers a key locution, the word "crisscross" uttered as Bruno offers his plan to Guy in the club car (9). Potentially the two men are exchangeable. Midway into the treatment when they meet after the murder, Guy insists that before Bruno told him he had murdered Miriam, he had not suspected him. Like Highsmith, Chandler protracts the time between their first meeting on the train and this second encounter, giving Guy plenty of time to put two and two together. Were Guy to acknowledge that he knew what Bruno did before Bruno told him, Guy would have to acknowledge something about himself—at the very least, that he wanted Miriam dead. He hides (from himself) how much he and Bruno are alike.

Chandler's Guy makes this clear when he insists to Bruno that he had no way of knowing that Bruno meant what he proposed on the train: "It could have been an act. You love to act. Your type always does" (65). "My type? What type?" Bruno returns in a stagy rejoinder, as if he didn't know what Guy was more than hinting. It takes one to know one; Guy's claims to total innocence also looks like an act. In Chandler, the two men trade closet performances. Then they get physical—Guy strikes Bruno, who responds by reiterating and intensifying his earlier line: "I like you so much." Perverse sexuality presumably thrives on such blows. "I like you better than anybody I've ever met," Bruno continues, "except my mother" (66). As Guy storms off, Bruno continues to insist how much he likes Guy and how much he wants to be his friend. "And the scene darkens and fades, leaving Bruno a harmless and whimpering little boy, whose feelings have been hurt. At that moment, you wouldn't think Bruno could have broken a doll, much less murdered a woman" (67).

At this moment, in Chandler's treatment, you know for sure what to make of Bruno. You can also suppose that the reason Bruno likes Guy so much is because they are so much alike. Instead, Chandler adds something in his treatment that is missing in Cook's, something that survives into the film: the scene in which Guy appears to go through with the bargain only to find Bruno in bed when he expected to find Bruno's father. "Crisscross" becomes "double cross" (90).

By this point in his treatment, Chandler registered the difficulty he was having writing it. With what William Luhr describes as a "relatively fixed notion of character" (1982, 84), Chandler found that he could not make the behavior of the two central characters psychologically plausible. He records his difficulty in his treatment, noting, for instance, that the more Bruno appears out in the open and the more he insists on being Guy's friend, the more unlikely it is that anyone will believe that he and Guy planned a murder that depended upon their not knowing each other. And the more Guy refuses to respond to Bruno, the more difficult it must be to sustain the possibility that Guy will go through with the bargain Bruno claims they struck on the train. Chandler remarks on the "logical weakness" of the original plot, claiming that it is "out of character" (79) for Guy to go through with the murder. Beyond that, Guy's behavior, for Chandler, is the product of muddled thinking. He should have been able to see that Bruno's self-destructive behavior was ruining the plot he had set in motion, killing any chance that anyone would believe that Guy had killed Miriam.

Having made these points in his treatment, Chandler has Guy make them to Bruno. Then, to make matters worse, having pointed out to Bruno the flaw in his supposed hold over him, Guy nonetheless agrees to go through with the murder exchange. Chandler thus goes out of his way to make the characters' behavior unbelievable.[3] Chandler's problem with visualizing was simply that he didn't believe that a film's visual logic could overcome such implausibility. As he wrote to Hitchcock: "I think you may be the sort of director who thinks that camera angles, stage business, and interesting bits of byplay will make up for any amount of implausibility in a basic story. And I think you are quite wrong" (MacShane 1981, 244). In notes on *Strangers on a Train,* Chandler further commented that what a reader might accept a character doing in a book is harder to sustain when the character appears on a screen (LaValley 1972, 101–4).

Chandler's viewers are naïvely supposed to believe they

---

3. Carringer suggests that Chandler's troubles with the script stem from his having been "charged" with creating his detective Marlowe as a closet "case" (2001, 376).

are seeing real people on screen moving in a real world. The visual is, for him, what is really visible as well as what is logically and rationally consistent. Hence Chandler dropped from his treatment, as well as from the screenplay he went on to write, one of the most striking visual moments from Cook's treatment, the reflection of the murder in Miriam's glasses. However, most of the other signature shots remain, although he did remove the crucial lighter-in-the-drain sequence, presumably because he found it implausible. In Chandler's treatment, Bruno manages to plant the lighter, but then gives away the fact that he did so in a final scene in the police station where he offers contradictory testimony about how he came to discover that Guy had left the lighter behind. Bruno's father appears in this scene to tell Guy that he should have come to him at the start, that he would have handled the whole thing. Bruno's father is Chandler's mouthpiece for a rationality that would have made the whole plot impossible; rational guys don't want to kill fathers. By the end, the treatment assumes this paternal position and has chosen to refuse all likeness between Guy and Bruno.

The difficulties Chandler had can be connected to the decision that Hitchcock and Cook made to begin with to break Highsmith's symmetry; Guy does not go through with the deal (however unconscious) he and Bruno struck on the train. Chandler's treatment highlights this, as does the screenplay he delivered to the studio on August 25, 1950. There has been a good deal of tightening in this version; we get to the scene where Bruno tells Guy about Miriam's murder much more expeditiously. Some new lines appear in the screenplay that Ormonde preserved. In the initial conversation on the train: "There I go again. Too friendly. I meet someone I like and admire and I open my yap too wide" (5); in their second conversation, when Bruno tells Guy what he has done and gives him Miriam's glasses: "You crazy fool"; "I like you, Guy" (46). But, as in his treatment, Chandler agonizes over the impossibility of making the plot plausible and has his characters speak what is on his own mind. Guy, for example, says that since he is a local celebrity, the fact that no one saw him in Metcalf the night Miriam was murdered is proof he wasn't there—he needs no alibi. In Chandler's screenplay, he's never a suspect. Once again, Guy tells Bruno that he has destroyed any chance for committing a perfect murder precisely by coming out in the open and by acting like a maniac at the Senator's party. Who would possibly believe him? What hold could he have over Guy? Once again Guy then pretends to go through with the deal, only to have Bruno tell him that he never believed Guy would do it, since he virtually told him he wouldn't. By the end of the screenplay, Guy tells Anne that Bruno will evade the force of the law only because "they can't hang a lunatic" and then feebly concludes, "One thing Bruno and I have in common, after all—I don't like merry-go-rounds any more" (143). For the sake of making the characters plausible, Chandler's initial screenplay undermines the projected film, undermines the likeness he brilliantly captured in the opening sequence of feet, and undermines the likeness that persists even when Guy does not go through with the exchange of murders. Ormonde preserved more of Chandler's script than is usually claimed; however, with Hitchcock and others continually revising, a final screenplay was produced that adhered closely to Cook's original treatment. The design of the film, when crisscross becomes double cross, is the juicy terrain of queer complication that I will be following in this book.

Censored endings: A final script ... or two?
There is, however, one further twist in the history of the script that bears on questions of queer sexuality in *Strangers on a Train*. As Bill Desowitz first discussed in a brief essay some twenty years ago, there are two versions of the film. The second version of *Strangers on a Train*—apparently an earlier version than the one finally released—first surfaced in the 1970s. Warner Bros. wanted to reissue the film: "[S]ince the original negative had been physically damaged they decided to utilize the best source available: a United Kingdom release print containing 'alternative footage and dialogue more British in tone'" (Desowitz 1992, 4). A 1979 Warner Bros. DVD release with the two versions on either side of the disk calls one of them the British print, so presumably Warner Bros. offered this account about the provenance of the alternative, earlier version. It runs some two minutes longer than the final US release. The 1979 video

FIGURE 6. Chandler doubles. DVD still.

quotes Desowitz on the jacket about the effect of this extra footage: "a startling amplification of Bruno's flamboyance, his homoerotic attraction to Guy and his psychotic personality."

Desowitz locates this increased homosexual emphasis particularly in the additional shots and dialogue to be found in the initial conversations on the train between Bruno and Guy, first in the club car and afterwards in Bruno's compartment. When Bruno credits his recognition of Guy—and knowledge of his relationship with Anne Morton—to his newspaper reading, Guy responds sardonically on how avid a reader

Bruno is. In lines that exist only in the earlier version, Bruno goes on to say that his newspaper reading embraces the stock report, the sports page, and even *Li'l Abner*. We see Bruno trying hard to ingratiate himself with Guy.

There are some visual ironies in this exchange about Bruno's reading habits worth noting here. It was Guy, after all, who was reading a book when Bruno first accosted him, one that has Hitchcock's picture on the back cover (Miller 2010, 110–13). There is no sign in their encounter in the club car that Bruno is a reader. However, in Bruno's compartment, a small stack of books can be spotted on the ledge beside the banquette on which Bruno sits and lounges. The books piled there consist of two copies of Raymond Chandler's *Finger Man* on top of Georgette Heyer's *Footsteps in the Dark*. These two books by Chandler can be added to the film's many doubles, a topic to which I will return in the final chapter of this book.[4] Miller has discerned that Hitchcock is responsible for the book that serves as Bruno's footrest; obliquely (in books all but invisible to the viewer), the tussle between the director and his fired writer gets played out again. Hitchcock also gets his face into scenes between the two men that Highsmith created, posing an almost invisible assertion of authorial rivalry

4. These may be the two copies of stories by Chandler that Hitchcock had in his office and happily gave away years later in an anecdote McGilligan (2003, 449) recounts as Hitchcock's last word on his dealings with the writer. Miller has identified the book Guy is reading as *Alfred Hitchcock's Fireside Book of Suspense*; he found Hitchcock's *Suspense Stories* beneath Bruno's feet (2010, 117).

and control that crosses gender and sexuality.

Desowitz notes other small differences between these early scenes on the train. One exchange in the pre-release, not found in the standard version of the film, certainly supports his claims about heightened homosexual implication. It's the moment when Bruno, in his compartment with Guy, asserts that everyone is a potential murderer. Guy refuses to countenance the idea that useless people should simply be eliminated. This exchange can't help but remind the viewer of the superman theory voiced in *Rope* (Hitchcock, 1948) in much the same terms (there connected to two men who can be read as gay, and who have just murdered another man). In *Rope*, as here, the enunciation of a Nietzschean perspective is the credo of those who break with social convention; sexual nonconformists are in the forefront of this elite. This relationship between sexuality and antisocial behavior is one thing that makes Hitchcock (and Highsmith) so compelling for me.

Desowitz had first been struck by the stark difference in the endings of the two versions of *Strangers on a Train*. The Hollywood ending has Anne and Guy on a train. Guy is accosted by a clergyman who recognizes him. This time, to avoid a replay of the meeting with Bruno from going anywhere, Guy refuses to acknowledge who he is, and he and Anne get up and move seats. The pre-release version does not include this scene. Rather, it stays with Anne on the phone receiving the news from Guy that all is well in Metcalf; the murderer has been revealed and he is no longer suspected.

Anne gets an additional line, which serves as the last word in the film. Having indicated that Guy wants her to meet him and bring him a change of clothes, she ends by saying that he's told her he will look silly in his tennis togs. That line did not find its way into the final version, perhaps because it doesn't make much sense: Guy had already changed out of his tennis gear in the cab as he sped toward the train to Metcalf and his final showdown with Bruno.

Why was this meeting with the cleric on the train not the conclusion to the earlier pre-release version? The answer that Desowitz offers has to do with its supposed provenance as a UK version operating under different conditions of censorship. It is now assumed, however, that what Desowitz calls the British version of *Strangers on a Train* was a US pre-release print. This is what Bill Krohn claims in a commentary on the 2004 two-disc Warner Bros. release. Its jacket labels the two versions as a preview version and the final release. The "British" designation has been dropped from the jacket description (Ken Mogg is the only Hitchcock critic who still talks about a British version [2008, 121]).

Desowitz assumed that the version he found riskier and more revealing of Bruno's sexuality was possible only if intended for a British audience; conversely, he assumed that the minister had to be removed because he would have offended Anglican sensibilities. Gene D. Phillips has furthered these claims: the more flamboyant homosexual Bruno of the so-called British version could not have survived "the industry film censor" who "maintained that homosexuality was too strong a subject for American motion pictures" (2000, 214). As Phillips points out, the code explicitly forbade "sex perversion" in films. He goes on to say that "the British Board of Censors ... permitted a rather forthright treatment of the subject in films released in England" (ibid.). But if both versions of *Strangers on a Train* are US versions, what role did the Production Code Administration play?

The omission of the final scene with the minister was not a response to an imagined British censor, but was a cut demanded by the censor Phillips has in mind, Joseph I. Breen, Vice President of the Motion Picture Association of America and Director of the Production Code Administration. Breen objected to the final scene with the minister in a letter of November 22, 1950 (in the Warner Bros. Archives). He wrote that the scene could be allowed to stand only if somehow the minister was not treated comically. (Breen also demanded that the phrase "Thank God" be eliminated from the film as well as the word "Jeez," strictly forbidden by the Code; "Nuts" also had to go.) Breen was not just worried about sex; mocking religion or committing blasphemy was his concern as well. He certainly would not have countenanced homosexuality had he spotted it, but, as Krohn remarks, "the censor ... never seems to have noticed the character's sexuality" (2000, 117). The line about potential supermen having the right to kill people who get in their way is the kind of thing Breen did object to. Although this line is not mentioned in

FIGURE 7. Guy and Bruno "necking." DVD still.

the correspondence preserved in the Warner Bros. Archives, Breen did demand that the line in which Anne says she would have condoned Guy's involvement with killing Miriam be removed. That line does not appear in any version of the film.

The homoerotics of *Strangers on a Train* was apparently invisible to the censors. Various local boards, reviewing the film after its release, found nothing to object to on that account. What they did find objectionable is nonetheless worth noting since it does register the normative points of view of the various censors. Individual boards of censors, in states including Ohio and Maryland, and cities like

Milwaukee, Toronto, and Boston, demanded cuts from the film before it could be shown in those locales. Warner Bros. met those demands. The extraordinary consequence is that rather than there being two versions of the film, at the time of its release there were as many as required by local review boards. Cut from virtually all of these was Guy's line to Miriam, "Especially when you're going to have another man's baby" (pregnancy is unmentionable when it implies extra-marital sex). As frequently cut, however, was the scene of the strangling of Miriam reflected in her eyeglasses. Sex and violence, it seems, was what was found most disturbing. (Bits of the dialogue with Mrs Cunningham were cut for Ohio viewers, while Barbara's declaration that it would be wonderful to have someone love you enough to kill for you was also not heard there, nor in Maryland.) The US Department of the Navy demanded removal of Barbara's line that her father, as a US Senator, didn't mind a bit of scandal. These demands echo those voiced in the five letters to Warner Bros. sent by Breen as he received portions of the film as it was being shot in October and November of 1950.[5] The dialogue with Miriam was found particularly objectionable for its "unacceptable" representation of marriage, although Breen went on to say that so long as the film made Miriam, not Guy, responsible

---

5. These letters, dated October 9 and November 7, 13, 15, and 22, are in the Warner Bros. Archives. An October 27 memo in the Margaret Herrick Library indicates the studio's agreement to rewrite the scene between Guy and Miriam to make her entirely responsible for the divorce.

for the failure of the marriage that would remove his worries. The Studio complied.

In Breen's caveat, it's easy to see the censor's desire to maintain Guy's role as a normative paradigm of masculinity, a role easily compatible with misogyny. But put together with Breen's other major concern about the film—the intense brutality of the final fight between Guy and Bruno on the merry-go-round, which he also found "unacceptable"—his objection may subliminally register a discomfort with a male-male intensity that exceeded the normative contours of male bonding. Breen explicitly asked that Bruno kicking Guy's knuckles be cut. He may well have been responding to what's hard not to miss (although never acknowledged by him)—how often in their final struggle the two men attempt to strangle each other. Strangling in these shots resonates with earlier moments in the film, of course, in which Bruno strangles Miriam or Mrs Cunningham or (in his imagination) Barbara. Strangling is erotically charged, most clearly when Bruno's pick-up line to Miriam leads to their fatal embrace, and it is almost as evident in the party scene at Senator Morton's where Bruno engages several matrons in a discussion about how unhappily married women might want to get rid of their husbands. The worry of the censors about representations about marriage and violence—their desire for a heteronormative point of view akin to the highly idealized pictures of marriage that one easily associates with the 1950s (*Ozzie and Harriet*, for example)— sits oddly with Hitchcock's film, to be sure.

Some of Breen's initial demands were met, and parts of the script he wanted gone did in fact wind up on the cutting room floor. The stamping of Guy's knuckles survived. How to explain this? Each of Breen's letters ends with a formula sentence which, it would seem, was not entirely rhetorical: "You understand, of course, that our final judgment will be based on the finished picture." The February 7, 1951 certificate of approval (on file in the Margaret Herrick Library), indicates that Breen had been assured that "the scenes of Robert Walker kicking at Farley Granger's hands have been reduced to a minimum" (likewise the choking of Mrs Cunningham). Presumably, the minister did not finally look like a joke to Breen. It's safe to suppose that he never imagined the final scene with the minister on the train as another possible pickup since he hadn't registered it as such in the initial encounter—in either version—of *Strangers on a Train*.

Cast calls and newspaper reviews

The role of Barbara was undoubtedly written with Patricia Hitchcock in mind; I'll have a final word to say about her queer part to end this book. For the role of Anne Morton, despite his desires (rumored to have fastened on Grace Kelly), Hitchcock had to employ Ruth Roman, under contract to Warner Bros. No one has had much to say for her contribution to the film. Nonetheless, like his favorite blondes, she is one of a number of female leads notable for an icy demeanor. In conversation with Truffaut, Hitchcock named William

Holden as his first choice for the role of Guy Haines, invidi-
ously comparing him to Farley Granger: "he's stronger" (1983,
199). Maybe so, but Holden had just played the gigolo and
talking corpse in Gloria Swanson's comeback vehicle *Sunset
Boulevard* (Billy Wilder, 1950), which might have made his
machismo just a bit equivocal. Even if Wilder's film was not
yet a camp classic, Holden's playing a kept man might have
been more what Hitchcock had in mind in wanting him for
the part. For, as Bosley Crowther remarked in a review of
Strangers on a Train that appeared in *The New York Times* on
July 4, 1951, like *Rope* before it, the film is an exercise in "the
Svengali theme" (1951A, 13).

In his earlier film, Hitchcock presented "a psychopathic
murderer who induced another young man to kill for thrills,"
Crowther went on to say in the review. He neglected to mention that Farley Granger played the impressionable young
man in both films. Initially Hitchcock may have had another
actor in mind for Guy. Nonetheless, Granger was not under
contract to Warner Bros.; he was not forced upon the director
by the Studio. Insofar as Hitchcock wanted to allow for the
possibility that Guy might indeed go through with Bruno's
plan to swap murders, it perhaps helped to choose an actor
who had been seduced to murder before. Indeed, Granger
specialized a bit in that kind of role. In Nicholas Ray's noir
They Live by Night (1949), as in Anthony Mann's *Side Street*
(1950), Granger's role depicts his unwilling involvement in a
world of tough male crime from which he can escape only

through his love for a woman. This is, more or less, the plot of Hitchcock's *Strangers on a Train*. In *Rope*, Granger plays a somewhat unwilling accomplice to John Dall's Brandon. Nonetheless, the film opens with the scene of the murder of David Kentley, and it is Granger who is tightening the noose around his neck. The combination of his ability to do it with his nervous, guilty, wound-up behavior, his at times hysterical repudiation of what he's done, made Granger apt for the part of Guy.

Comparison to *Rope* also underscores the confluence of a murder plot with a homosexual plot, indeed the virtual transposition of one upon the other. Arthur Laurents, who wrote the screenplay for *Rope*, remarks in an interview quoted in Vito Russo's *The Celluloid Closet* that although no one mentioned homosexuality while *Rope* was being filmed, Hitchcock surely understood the nature of Brandon and Phillip's relationship, as well as the homosexuality of their former teacher Rupert Cadell: "If you asked Hitchcock, he'd tell you it isn't there, knowing perfectly well it is" (Russo 1987, 94; Laurents makes the same point in an interview available in the Laurent Bouzereau documentary *"Rope" Unleashed* [2000] found on the current Universal DVD release of *Rope*). Rupert had induced his former prep school students to believe that extraordinary people had the right to dispose of useless people. This is the line that disappeared from Bruno's mouth in the final release of *Strangers on a Train*. James Stewart, who played the part of Rupert, reportedly never understood that he

FIGURE 8. Granger cheesecake on the set. Photofest.

was the gay mentor to the murderers and, as such, bore some responsibility for a murder committed to prove his theory. Such obtuseness (about sexuality, about criminality) figures as well in *Strangers on a Train*. When leaving Bruno's compartment, Guy appears to agree with Bruno, who says that they speak the same language; he appears to be engaged in an unwitting act of homosexual recognition. So Richard Barrios suggests in *Screened Out*, finding it apt since "*Strangers* is as gleefully insidious about Bruno's homosexuality as Bruno himself is about, well, everything" (2003, 228). Another sign that Hitchcock knew what was going on—that is, knew without saying that *Rope* carried homosexual innuendos (at the very least)—is that, according to Laurents, Hitchcock had hoped to have Cary Grant play the part that went to Stewart and had wanted Montgomery Clift to play one of the young men. Grant and Clift refused because they too understood the risk entailed in taking these parts: they might be outed.

Granger presumably was not worried, but not because he was straight. He and Laurents were lovers while Granger was working on *Rope*. In his nicely titled autobiography, *Include Me Out*, whose title refers not only to his sexuality but also to his opting out of the studio system, Granger confirms what Laurents says—that there was no talk of homosexuality on the set; he adds, however, that he and Laurents certainly discussed it. As McGilligan opines, it's a nice "crisscross" in the casting of *Strangers on a Train* that Robert Walker, who he assumes was straight, played a presumptively gay character to Granger's supposedly straight Guy (2003, 451). Parker Tyler makes the same point, wondering whether Hitchcock chose a gay actor for Guy precisely to play on the closeted

FIGURE 9. Call Me Madam. Photofest.

performance required by the studio and the censors, noting the additional dollop of sexual deliciousness as Bruno's plot turns to his stalking of Guy, revealing "the beautiful camp of the charade's other face," as the murder plot covers the homo-sexual one (1973, 184).

Certainly Warner Bros. was invested in not revealing a casting crisscross. Publicity shots have Granger hors-ing around with Shelley Winters—although Granger never claimed her as a romantic interest. Granger was promoted by Warner Bros. as a teen heartthrob. Shots of him in his tennis togs, with remarks about his legs, were part of the Studio promotional releases; in photo shoots for the January 23, 1951 issue of *Modern Screen*, Granger butches it up in his "bachelor hideaway," carrying logs "to keep the home fires burning," the caption beneath a bare-chested image declares. Indoors, however, we see Granger with his record collection fanned out on the floor. There's a classical item just visible—Satie—and a couple of show albums artfully strewn. One can just make out Mary Martin's name. However, the name most immediately legible is Ethel Merman, the show *Call Me Madam*. Ostensibly unknowingly, but maybe not, the studio's promotion of Granger had gay male appeal.

Early reviewers of the film did not notice the poten-tial crisscross in having Granger play Guy and Walker play Bruno. Crowther's mention of *Rope* is about as close as any journalist got. Philip Hartung, reviewing *Strangers on a Train* in *Commonweal* on July 20, 1951, might be described as hav-ing seen the film through Joseph Breen's eyes. He glimpsed something troubling about Guy. Among the "fishy aspects" of the plot for Hartung was Guy's being "in love with his boss's daughter while he is still tied to his tramp of a wife," as well as Guy's failure to go to the police immediately after Miriam is killed (1951, 358). This reviewer (like Bruno) suspects Guy's sexual behavior and doubts that his interest in Anne Morton is sexual; he underscores his guilt. Hartung stops short of the next step, however, never asking whether or how much Guy likes women at all. Sounding even more a censor, the unnamed reviewer in *The Christian Century* on August 8, 1951, perhaps predictably wrote that the "film is *interesting stylistically but deplorable* in theme, which depends on unwholesome concepts for ideas, artificial motivation for progress" (1951, 927; their emphasis).

Hartung refers to Bruno as a "neurotic young man" (1951, 358); most other reviewers go further. In the review we've cited already, Crowther reserves "psychopathic" for *Rope*'s Brandon, and describes Bruno as "weirdly unbalanced"; however, in a second *New York Times* review a few days later, he calls Bruno "a psychopathic killer"(1951B, 2, 1). "The villain is a queer, unbalanced fellow," he goes on to say. "Spoiled and, as it develops, psychotic" was the judgment of Hollis Alpert writing in *The Saturday Review* on July 14, 1951; he also labels him "paranoid" (32).

These reviewers say "homosexual" without saying it, much as scriptwriter Arthur Laurents describes the evasiveness in the production of *Rope* where everyone was in the know, but nobody said the word. Or, perhaps, this is how, in large measure, "homosexual" was said, in the reviewers' language

of pathology. Nonetheless, reviewer Manny Farber, writing in
The Nation on July 28, 1951, had no trouble saying the word.
Farber didn't much like *Strangers on a Train*, and one of the
things he didn't like was "the travestied homosexuality of the
murderer" (78). Farber, that is, not only saw Bruno as gay;
he also deplored the terms under which such recognition
was fostered: neurosis or psychosis, the young man "spoiled"
by his mother, the homosexual as killer. In this context, it's
worth mentioning that the character of Bruno's mother,
played so superbly by Marion Lorne, was in all likelihood
largely Czenzi Ormonde's invention. Instead of Chandler's
showgirl, Ormonde gives us a woman destroyed by a tyrant
husband, limited to reciting the empty rituals of her social
class. Rather than a woman who ruins her son, she is a woman
herself ruined.

Farber extends praise to Walker's performance of Bruno
and was especially drawn to Laura Elliott's Miriam. "The
heavy blanket of twisted melancholia which Walker spreads
over this film is beautifully counterpointed by the work of
Laura Elliott in the role of the victim ... All the best things
in 'Strangers' have to do with the playing of these two"
(ibid.).[6] Farber's praise of Elliott's acting is unusual, although

---

6. Farber returns to this point in his late-1960s piece "Clutter" (2009, 607), where
he joins praise of Elliott to deprecating remarks about the other female charac-
ters/actresses in the film. Under the name Kasey Rogers, Elliott appeared as Betty
Anderson's mother in hundreds of episodes of the 1960s television version of *Peyton
Place*.

Hitchcock also voices admiration for "the bitchy wife" in his discussion with Truffaut (1983, 198)—the misogyny in the film elicits far more energy than is generated by the respectable Anne. Farber's high estimation of Walker's performance is echoed in virtually every early review and most current critical remarks as well. Farber comments on Walker's transformation from a typecast "boy-next-door" to his performance as Bruno. In line with this metamorphosis, Granger reports that when Hitchcock offered him the role of Guy Haines, he also told him mischievously that he had signed Walker to the part of Bruno: "Wouldn't it be interesting if something happened on our film?" Granger claims Hitchcock said (2007, 108). What Hitchcock had in mind was the possibility of some sort of crack-up, Granger presumes.

Walker had been famously dumped by his first wife Jennifer Jones, who was involved sexually with David O. Selznick. He had a breakdown and was hospitalized. He had also been arrested for drunk driving; his booking photo, showing a disheveled Walker, had been published in *Life* magazine. These events might well have tarnished the boy-next-door appeal of Walker. In films like *One Touch of Venus* (William Seiter, 1948) and *The Clock* (Vincente Minnelli, 1945), there is a certain feyness in Walker's performances that Hitchcock might well have spied. Perhaps he hoped Walker might wear it (as he does) as the veneer over the kind of potentially out-of-control behavior that Walker had rather publicly put on display. Something like this is what Pauline Kael found in

FIGURE 10. Between Men. Publicity shot. Warner Bros. Pictures / Photofest.

Walker's performance of "dear degenerate Bruno," noting his "sportive originality... [and] chilling wit" that made his acting, rather than any feat of Hitchcock's directing, most memorable about the film (1991, 720). According to Granger, Walker's behavior on the set was above reproach. He claims Walker was late for only one shooting session after a bad night the two men spent together, Walker being distraught over Jones. Still, where Walker was headed is noted in Kael's review, which is retrospective praise of "the late Robert Walker." A month after *Strangers on a Train* opened, Walker's out-of-control behavior caused his psychiatrist to be called to his home where the doctor administered a sedative, to which Walker had what is usually described as a fatal allergic reaction.[7]

The Studio's publicity handled Walker's marital break-up and the psychological difficulties it caused him by presenting him as a family man, one who was spending much time with his two sons; plans for their time together was detailed. Preempting the possibility that anyone might identify Walker with Bruno, his "conservative" style was stressed in contrast

---

7. Beverly Linet more plausibly reports that the drug had been administered to Walker many times before, but was counter-indicated given his alcoholism; the result of its administration was instant respiratory failure (1986, 272–73). She also indicates that besides a doctor or two or possibly three, present at this scene was Walker's best friend Jim Henaghan. Given her Romeo and Juliet title (*Star-Crossed*), which allows Walker only a single sustained heterosexual interest (Jones), she does not go further about Henaghan; he is often represented in Linet's story as a drinking companion and someone who provided Walker with dates. However, he is quoted saying: "a lot of people in this town thought we were a couple of fags … If there is such a thing as love, I loved Bobby, … but there were a lot of perverted minds that couldn't accept the fact that two men could love each other without being sexual deviates" (1986, 220).

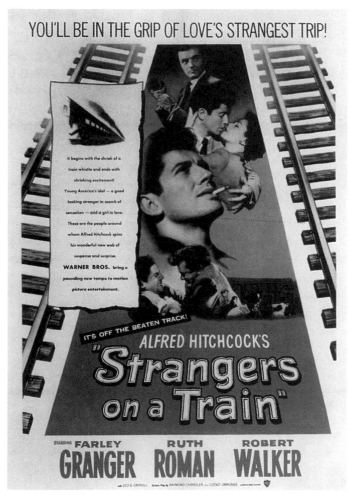

FIGURE 11. Love's Grip—around the throat. Poster. Warner Bros. Pictures / Photofest.

with Bruno's, who is described as "a charming cosmopolite, an introvert who deliberately acts like an extrovert, masking an evil, warped mind." Walker, this November 17, 1951 publicity release assured readers, was nothing like the character he played. The pop-psychology terminology hints at the "flamboyant" homosexuality of Bruno, as does the emphasis on sartorial details—Walker himself doesn't dress in the flashy style of Bruno; no lobster ties or silk dressing gowns or sporty shoes for him. With similar ends in mind, publicity stills for *Strangers on a Train* often posed the stars in triangular configurations showing Roman, Granger, and Walker. These shots might have suggested that the film was about two men struggling over a woman but can be read another way, of course, as our initial glimpse at "the three Hitchcocks" suggested; in the film, Bruno wants Guy for himself, or perhaps (as is even more overtly the case in Highsmith's novel) wants to insinuate himself into the relationship. One publicity poster teases with punning promises: the film is "off the beaten track" and it promises, "You'll be in the Grip of Love's Strangest Trip!"

Were the studio's efforts to dispel any thoughts that Walker might be like Bruno further motivated? What was Walker's sexuality? Was he simply the star-crossed lover of Beverly Linet's account of his relationship with Jennifer Jones? In Darwin Porter's recent unauthorized biography of Merv Griffin, Griffin is said to have had three-way sex with Walker and Peter Lawford several times (2009, 56, 98, 143) as well as a brief affair with Walker (ibid., 141–42). The book also claims that Lawford and Walker sometimes had sex together with Nancy Davis, the future Mrs Ronald Reagan. The biographer does not claim that Walker was exclusively gay—affairs with Judy Garland and Ava Gardner, with whom he had starred in the best of his boy-next-door films, also are mentioned. (Granger, too, claims to have had a fling with Gardner.) About his performance of Bruno, Walker is reported to have told Merv Griffin "that he was playing a homicidal homosexual…: 'Farley and I will know we're playing it homo, but only the hip ones in the audience will get it,'" he reportedly said (ibid., 100). Laurents too claims that "Farley Granger told me once that it was Robert Walker's idea to play Bruno Antony as a homosexual" (Russo 1987, 94), a point not made in Granger's autobiography, however. Donald Spoto credits Walker and Hitchcock for coming up with a way of playing the part gay that would elude the censors. Was Walker perhaps playing himself playing Bruno? Lawford is supposed to have found sex with Walker particularly thrilling: "It's the feeling that with him you never know what's going to happen next, including the possibility that he's going to commit suicide at any moment," the Griffin biographer quotes him as having said (ibid., 136).

Hollywood gossip about Walker may well not have been true, or it may have been. It certainly might have been circulating at the time *Strangers on a Train* was being filmed. We've seen that reviewers were mesmerized by Walker's stunning performance, how they said without saying what they made of the character of Bruno. The reviewers were all but unanimous, too, in complaining that Hitchcock's film offered "Dexterity in a Void," to quote the title of Bosley Crowther's second *New York Times* review. In his earlier review he complained about what he called Hitchcock's "touches," concluding, "Frankly, we feel that Mr. Hitchcock is 'touching' us just a bit too much." Crowther, that is, cast Hitchcock himself as a "Svengali," working his effects on the audience. "Facileness and artificiality" were what was on offer, Hollis Alpert complained in the *Saturday Review*, much as he did about "spoiled" Bruno, that mama's boy. "Gimmicks" was all the picture amounted to, Nathaniel Benchley chimed in (1951, 28). "Scene after scene is jammed with Hitchcock tricks that leave you limp with excitement," film critic Hartung complained in *Commonweal* (1951, 359), a sentiment much like the one Brandon voices in *Rope* about the pleasure he felt over David Kentley's spent body.

What are these reviewers saying? Perhaps something like what Arthur Laurents claims about the technical "trick" of *Rope*, which pretends to be shot without cuts and then hides the cuts in plain view (much as, D.A. Miller argues, it displays homosexuality without ever saying it). The forthright Manny Farber comes closest to saying what these accounts of Hitchcock's gimmicks are all but saying when he complains about "the general emasculation Hitchcock has perpetrated on the thriller" (1951, 78). Farber, who liked the sexual tension between Bruno and Miriam (and imagined tough guy Chandler to be responsible for it, not an entirely mistaken assumption), deplored the most famous shot in the film, the strangling supposedly reflected in Miriam's eyeglasses. This is, of course, an "effect" produced by complex camera work and filming. "At once the onlooker loses interest in the murder as such because he is so entranced with the lush, shadowy choreographic lyricism with which Hitchcock shows the life being squeezed, fraction by fraction, out of a shallow, hateful nymphomaniac" (ibid.). Even as he denounces the visual effects, Farber registers their "touch" in quite extraordinary prose. He sees the film turning murder into an art. He also sees in Hitchcock's aesthetics, that is, something akin to what Brandon enunciates in *Rope*, that murder is an art. Hitchcock, it hardly needs to be said, is not a naturalistic director. The critics deplored in *Strangers on a Train* what Thomas Elsaesser has termed Hitchcock's dandyism. It's part of what we might want to name—and what his reviewers all but did—his queerness. It helps make *Strangers on a Train* a queer classic.

TWO: CRITICAL INTERLUDES

Strangers on a Train has not gotten as much critical attention as some other widely acclaimed Hitchcock films—*Vertigo* (1958), *Psycho* (1960), or *The Birds* (1963), for instance. Yet, if only because of the part of Bruno Antony, it has been important in the discussion or, at the very least, mention of homosexuality and Hitchcock. Donald Spoto, for instance, alludes to "an implicit element, the homosexual theme" (1976, 209) in the film. His casual remark becomes more interesting when he continues by suggesting that it "must have been considered quite shocking to some in 1951" (ibid.). A contradiction in Spoto's words provides one focus in this chapter: how can the homosexual theme be "implicit" and yet be shocking? Spoto's plot summary offers a possible answer: "*Strangers* may be seen as the demonic courtship of a latent homosexual by a psychopathic killer" (1976, 218). "Latent homosexual" has a wonderfully antiquated air about it, a remnant of a pop Freudianism that has not had much shelf value. If Guy is "latent," Bruno, presumably, is "blatant," a "psychopathic killer" whose courtship of a man makes him a "shocking" homosexual. That kind of pathologizing claim has drawn charges of homophobia.

This chapter does not aim to survey all the critical works on *Strangers on a Train* that mention homosexuality. I want rather to focus on this criticism insofar as it can enable a reading of the film as a queer classic. There has yet to be a full-scale queer reading of *Strangers on a Train*: this book aims to provide one. Lee Edelman, D. A. Miller, and Leo Bersani provide inspiring models of what that reading would look like as this chapter moves to its conclusion.

Hitchcock's homophobia

The French new wave filmmakers Eric Rohmer and Claude Chabrol's 1957 book on Hitchcock (available in English since 1979) offers an account of homosexuality in *Strangers on a Train* that has proven influential. They situate the film as the third in a homosexual "triptych" that includes *Murder!* (1930) and *Rope* (1948), "a triptych that illustrates the problem of homosexuality from three points of view: moral in *Murder!*, realistic in *Rope*, and psychoanalytic in *Strangers on a Train*" (1979, 27). Homosexuality, for these critics, is a "vice," and they take the three films to demonstrate "the impossibility of true homosexual love" (1979, 27–28). In "Hitchcock's Homophobia," an article that first appeared in *Christopher Street* in 1982, John Hepworth seized on Rohmer and Chabrol to make a case against Hitchcock.[8] "Gay sexuality was his supreme bête noire," Hepworth writes: "Hitch was a supreme fag baiter" (1995, 188). Just as reprehensible, in his view, are "critics

---

8. Hepworth's essay is more easily found now in the "Dossier on Hitchcock" in Corey Creekmur and Alexander Doty's important 1995 compilation, *Out in Culture*.

FIGURE 12. Flamboyant Bruno tortures sweet Anne. DVD still.

like Robin Wood, Eric Rohmer, or Claude Chabrol," who "condone his homophobia" (1995, 189).

Hepworth's evidence for the homophobia of *Strangers on a Train* amounts to two examples: "Try sitting through the scene in which *sweet* Ruth Roman pleads with bitchy, *sadistic* Robert Walker (wearing a flamboyant dressing gown) without getting a bit hot under the collar. Or listen as Walker, all diabolical sultriness...cruises Farley Granger with such prissy gems as 'I've had a *strenuous* evening' and 'I'm afraid I don't know what a *smoocher* is'" (1995, 189).

We can put aside the smoocher line, which comes from an entirely different moment in the film; it is not directed at Guy and is not a scene of cruising, either. What is Hepworth's case? As Alexander Doty points out in his introduction to the "Hitchcock Dossier" in *Out in Culture*, Hepworth seeks "positive images" (1995, 194) and lambastes Hitchcock for deploying the kinds of negative stereotypes readily found in the media that represent homosexuals as murderers, molesters or, at the very least, mentally disturbed.

For Hepworth, one stereotype that rankles is Walker's feminization: he is "bitchy" and "prissy," a mix of sultry seductiveness and coy refusal. Moreover, he is sadistic—this is Hepworth's diagnosis, delivered in italics—as he plays with his victim, "*sweet* Ruth Roman." And he is evil: as bad as his "sinful passion for Farley Granger" (1995, 193) is his untoward cruising of an innocent straight man. Hepworth would like gay Bruno to be represented as kind to women, but not because homosexuals are like women. Moreover, gay men should be respectful of straight men, not cruising them. Finally, it seems that for Hepworth, representations of gay men should be indistinguishable from normative men: they shouldn't be portrayed as "flamboyant."

No one wants to see gay men always represented as evil, of course, but I have to ask: isn't the Bruno that Hepworth desires as disturbing as the negative stereotype? Doesn't it depend on normative gender behavior? Would Hepworth's ideal gay man be one of those "straight acting, straight appearing" gay men that used to be a feature in the sex ads, which these days stress "masculinity" as a desired trait? Isn't his "positive image" of a gay man an idealization based in a heterosexual norm? And isn't Hitchcock's Bruno—and Robert Walker's performance of the part—a lot more than a stereotype? We can enjoy Walker's performance (I certainly do) without feeling that homosexuals are being maligned.

This brings me to the way Hepworth calls the characters in the film by the names of the actors playing the parts. By doing that, the distance between reality and representation disappears. In something of the same way, when Rohmer and Chabrol characterize homosexuality as a "problem," they use a sociological term of analysis, as if Hitchcock's film might be an intervention to clear up a social dilemma, or as if it directly represented a pressing social situation. A similar but perhaps even more overstated collapse occurs when Hepworth describes Vito Russo's project in *The Celluloid Closet* as showing "the rivers of gay blood that Hollywood" has on its hands (1995, 193). Hepworth's statement turns Hollywood footage into actual slaughter, as if representations killed people.

Reality certainly is related to representation but, I would insist, the relationship is neither one-to-one nor causal. Films don't immediately reflect anything, not even the actors being filmed. Homophobia is arguably endemic to modern western culture; still, to credit society—or films—as such successful mechanisms of oppression is to overstate the case. It is to subscribe to a vision of power that places it always in anyone's hands but our own. I see no political advantage in taking such a position.

I would suggest, moreover, that what can get lost in such

FIGURE 13. Bruno "necking", Barbara coming into view. DVD still.

a view is the work that film does as film. Even Rohmer and Chabrol can contribute more to the understanding of homosexuality in Hitchcock than their invidious triptych does. Despite their deplorable views, they offer us a way to negotiate the distance between reality and representation. In analyzing *Strangers on a Train*, they do not concentrate on its role in their triptych; rather, they are fascinated by the film's formal structure. They schematize that structure as the relationship between the straight line and the circle. They regard this geometry as the formal reflection of a central theme of Hitchcock's films—their exchanges and transfers—especially

FIGURE 14. Crisscross. DVD still.

the transfer of guilt. This theme is at the heart of the relationship between Guy and Bruno: it is Guy who is assumed guilty by the police who tail him, Bruno who is not suspected until the very end of the film. Rohmer and Chabrol conclude their book with a discussion of *The Wrong Man* (1957) as the Hitchcock film that consolidates this theme. The point about the wrong man—the man wrongly accused of the crime—is that he is virtually indistinguishable from the right man, the criminal. If a straight line always heads in one direction and keeps to its own distinct path, the circle does not. Right and wrong might not be distinct.

In *Strangers on a Train*, we may suppose a complete difference between Bruno and Guy, gay and straight, guilty and innocent. But from the opening sequence on, Hitchcock plays a game of sameness and difference. Parallel shot follows parallel shot as we move from Bruno's legs and shoes to Guy's. At the same time, the feet face each other and seem to be heading toward each other. As mirror images, they face in opposite directions. And, of course, we would never mistake the footgear of one for the other, even though it might make more sense for them to be in each other's shoes. The circles in the film—among them the merry-go-round that runs amok, the eyeglasses in which the murder is reflected, or the woman's neck that is so enticing—produce vertigo, as Rohmer and Chabrol stress: Bruno faints. We see the murder through a cracked and distorted lens. We experience a kind of vertigo, too, viewing the shots that open the film; are we to distinguish between Guy and Bruno or not? The railways tracks run parallel, then cross. The straight line bends and curves.

Rohmer and Chabrol's "straight" is not meant sexually; nonetheless, I think we can read it that way. When they conclude their discussion, they bring the formal features of the film into proximity with the "taints" of Bruno—including his "sexual perversion"—to conclude, however, that "Bruno's criminal attitude is only a debased form of an attitude basic to all human beings. In his sickness we can distinguish—corrupted, perverted, but given a kind of esthetic dignity—the very archetype of all our desires" (1979, 110). Rohmer and

Chabrol may believe that what they take to be Bruno's homosexuality marks him as sick, perverted, and corrupt. But they also link his "debasement" to a more general human condition. They insist that he is linked to anyone, to everyone. In moving between a view that stigmatizes Bruno as gay and one that sees him as akin to anyone else, they confront and enact one of the impasses that Eve Kosofsky Sedgwick identified in *Epistemology of the Closet*. Endemic to modern western culture, she argues, is this question: Are homosexuals a distinct minority or not? If not, the difference between straight and gay always will be a fraught site, a place of crossing rather than a line firmly drawn between.

"We are as much on his [Bruno's] side as we are on Guy's. It's all a back and forth motion, a crossing over," Rohmer and Chabrol contend (1979, 110). If "we," in this sentence, are presumed not to be Bruno, we can't simply be Guy either, since "we" move back and forth. The film insists on their doubling even as it seeks to keep them distinct. Doing so, it makes possible our mobile identifications. In crossing back and forth, Rohmer and Chabrol suggest, we are led to a recognition of sameness. This is not, for them, the sameness of a norm or of the normal. For them, human guilt makes us all alike. I don't find myself very drawn to such theological terms, and prefer to see their claims through what Leo Bersani posits, "'the homo' in all of us" (1995, 10). Rohmer and Chabrol, moreover, attribute these effects of mobile identification to the aesthetics of the film. Richard Allen remarks on such features as "the patterned doubling" of *Strangers on a Train*: "Hitchcock's bravura style…expresses in its purely formal, geometric terms the love that otherwise dare not speak its name" (2007, 146). The formal features, in other words, create "homo" similarity that overrides whatever "moral" distinctions the film may seem to endorse.

Hitchcock is clearly invested in Bruno as the vital engine of his design. If Hepworth can succumb to what he takes to be Martin Landau's gay performance in *North by Northwest* (1959)—when he is at his "sneaky creepy best" (1995, 189)—I don't see why Bruno should bother him so much. Indeed, Rohmer and Chabrol contend that this is what Hitchcock got from his performers (not least Robert Walker): "we…rediscover not only the same mannerisms in actors as different as George Sanders in *Rebecca* and Robert Walker in *Strangers on a Train*: the same astonished eyebrows, the same sulking pout, the same half-homosexual, half-childish affectations" (1979, 60). "The seductive Uncle Charlie will have as his cousins the Brandon of *Rope* and the Bruno Anthony of *Strangers on a Train*" (1979, 73). Far beyond the narrow confines of an invidious homosexual triptych, if still in terms we may deplore, Rohmer and Chabrol open Hitchcock's work to a homosexuality without limits. Rather than a world of persecuted gays, Hitchcock would seem instead to offer queer films, displaying not so much a minoritarian logic as a queer universalism (to recall again the categories developed by Sedgwick). It's there, I think, that we can take our pleasure in Hitchcock.

FIGURE 15. Bruno's watch. DVD still.   FIGURE 16. On Guy's wrist. DVD still.

The Homosexual Menace

Questions about the relationship of films to reality are central to Robert J. Corber's reading of *Strangers on a Train* in *In the Name of National Security: Hitchcock, Homophobia, and the Political Construction of Gender in Postwar America*. I cite the full title because it all but states the thesis of his book: Hitchcock's films replicate their historical era, in particular the worry that the US government was being infiltrated by homosexuals who were subject to blackmail and therefore represented security risks to the state.[9] This paranoid claim had real effects:

---

9. Carringer dismisses Corber's reading on narrow, literalistic grounds (2001, 373, because the Senate report, *The Employment of Homosexuals and Other Sex Perverts in Government* [Washington, DC: Government Printing Office, 1950], postdates the film, there can be no coincidence between them, and in order to support a view of authorship which, whatever its putative claims to be collaborative, are for him ultimately quite individualistic. Attributing entirely to Hitchcock something which must also have been a historical possibility, he endorses *Strangers on a Train* as a "sweepingly transgressive" film for its time for its ambiguous (rather than obviously stigmatizing)

FIGURE 17. Guy and Bruno behind bars. DVD still.   FIGURE 18. Capital shot. DVD still.

men and women assumed to be gay lost their jobs and had their careers ruined. The persecution of suspected gays went hand in hand with the search for Communists. This makes a certain kind of sense for Corber: the gays he admires were on the left; they understood themselves as an oppressed minority, like blacks or women. Corber contrasts these progressive gays to those who insisted that they were no different from any other upstanding citizen except in terms of what they did in bed. Their sexual behavior, they insisted, made no difference.

It is, Corber contends, precisely in this area of difference/ no difference where the heart of his story lies. Had it been obvious who was gay, the government would have had no problem identifying and eliminating gays. Corber sees an analogous strategy at work in the way *Strangers on a Train*

---

representations of male-male relations that could be construed as gay (2001, 377). That final point I am quite happy to endorse.

FIGURE 19. Bruno at the Jefferson Memorial. DVD still.

frequently produces uncanny effects of identity-in-differ-
ence, identity at a distance. Bruno need only consult his
watch for Guy to look at his, although miles away (but in the
very next shot). When Bruno tells Guy that he has murdered
Miriam, matching shots place each man behind bars, both
the one who is technically guilty and the one who technically is not. In such moments, the film translates the specter
of the homosexual menace, the threat that no visible difference will secure difference. Hence, when Corber writes
that "Hitchcock's film ratifies the findings of the Senate's
Appropriations Committee" (1993, 78)—the committee had

spent 1950 gathering testimony and writing a report—he points to the committee's conclusion that "sexual identities are fluid and unstable, straights are incapable of resisting the sexual advances of gay men and lesbians" (ibid.). Corber takes Hitchcock to be as invested as the US Senate in showing the ghastly truth of the homosexual menace, a homophobic project no different from what was taking place in the Capitol.

The strongest point in favor of this thesis lies in something Corber rightly stresses, the Washington, DC location of the film. Highsmith's *Strangers on a Train* is not set there; her Guy's new love is not a US senator's daughter. In the opening shot of the film, the dome of the Capitol looms on the horizon. The establishing shot establishes where we are, something we are not allowed to forget, as when we see Bruno as the dark blob on the steps of the Jefferson Memorial menacing Guy just as he tells Hennessey about his political ambitions.

Hitchcock certainly places the film in a political context. Does that mean that it replicates or supports the homophobic policies of the US government, as Corber contends? Barbara's line about "Daddy" not minding a little scandal offended the government because of its flippant attitude toward senatorial morality. Guy's future ambitions cast in doubt whether he loves Anne or is indeed intent on marrying the boss's daughter. "Politics," in such a view, is little more than personal ambition, scarcely a beacon of moral probity. The party at Senator Morton's, with wives ready to imagine killing their husbands, gives further pause to the film's supposed

investment in reason of state. In that scene, Bruno's performance, as he spouts absurd theories to politicians who are
used to entertaining them, seems part and parcel of political
life. Soon they'll be talking about orgies. And when Bruno
challenges the callous judge who sends a man to death and
eats his dinner with a clear conscience, with whom does
the film ask us to identify? We may wonder whether setting
Strangers on a Train so centrally in the seat of government
signals Hitchcock's pledge of allegiance.

Moreover, as Corber contends, the possibility that supposed straights might be secret gays, that straight and gay
might not be so distinct, suggests that even if the film aimed
to wave the flag, slippage remains an inevitable possibility.
Indeed, Corber knows that Hitchcock treads in dangerous
waters when he seeks to solicit the gaze of the presumptively
straight male viewer by having him identify with Guy. When
does wanting to be like someone and identifying with him
become wanting to have him? Corber writes: "The process of
identification involves the repression of a potentially desta-
bilizing homosexual object cathexis between spectator and
hero. The male spectator must first desire the hero before
he can identify with him. The widespread paranoia with
respect to male heterosexual identities in postwar America
rendered this aspect of identification extremely problematic.
By encouraging the male spectator to identify with the hero,
Hitchcock's film threatened to reinforce his sexual insta-
bility" (1993, 81–82). Corber acknowledges the point I am

FIGURE 20. Guy's face, Bruno's hands. DVD still.

making—that sexuality cannot be controlled by representation—when he notes "the resistance of sexuality to containment through representation" (1993, 61). Nonetheless, he seems ultimately to believe that the film succeeds in making gay/straight difference distinct. This belief parallels Corber's belief that, faced with the power of the government, gays must be a distinct, oppressed minority.

Corber finally treats the homosexual menace in the film as a gender problem. For him, ultimately, the film's project is to maintain gender difference. This argument finds its counterpart in a contemporaneous essay by Sabrina Barton

FIGURE 21. Two imposters the same. (Guy and Bruno? Guy and Anne?). DVD still.

that initially appeared in *Camera Obscura* in 1991.[10] For her, *Strangers on a Train* is a product of "Hollywood's misogynistic and homophobic plotting" (1993, 242). As this pairing suggests, "the female and homosexual other" (1993, 243) are, for her, the same. Barton's interest in homophobia in the film is limited to its role as an analogue to its misogyny. Bruno is quickly understood by her as a "deranged homosexual"; what is of interest to Barton is his pairing with Miriam, the

10. An initial version of Corber's chapter on *Strangers on a Train* had appeared in *Discourse* in 1991. I'll be citing Barton's essay in its 1993 republication; it also can be found in Creekmur and Doty (1995, 216–38).

"voracious tramp" (1993, 237) who threatens Guy. Guy, at the center of the plot, is a beleaguered hero subject to "the film's hyperbolically Freudian and homophobic account of how the paranoid subject, suffering from the repression and distortion of homosexual desire, projects a persecuting double" (ibid.). To restate her argument: Bruno is Guy's double; by killing Miriam he enacts Guy's repressed homosexuality as well as his misogyny.

Barton goes no further in her Freudian analysis. In her account, Guy is an insecure man. But is he "really" gay? Barton does not say. She insists, rather, on the projection onto Bruno of desires Guy cannot own as his own. But, as she also demonstrates thoroughly, the camera works to produce Guy and Bruno as doubles. There is, as she notes, that extraordinary moment when Guy tells Anne on the phone that he could strangle Miriam; the next frame, momentarily superimposed on his utterance, shows Bruno's hands being manicured by his mother. Here, once again, is that uncanny coincidence of the two men, as if they were one, just as the first sequence of feet had set up what Barton, who offers an exacting shot-by-shot analysis, calls a "homosexual … symmetry" (1993, 237).

For Barton, the film is ultimately intent upon differentiating Guy from Bruno, normal from pervert. Despite all the symmetry involved in the late, extended sequence of parallel cross-cut shots between the tennis game and the sewer drain, Guy and Bruno are as starkly opposed as the blazing light that surrounds Guy in his whites and the dank and filthy place where Bruno reaches his murderous hand. Yet, as Barton also notes, the Forest Hills stadium sports a quotation from Kipling: "And treat those two imposters just the same" (1993, 250).

According to Barton, Hitchcock's film shows that Guy's normalcy is an "imposture … even as it subscribes to Freud's own investment in that imposture" (246). But if there is only imposture, there is no "normalcy." There is the visibility that leads Barton and others to see Bruno and say "homosexual," and there is the invisibility of those that lack whatever sign it is that triggers that response (a vocal inflection? a "flamboyant" dressing gown? a doting mother?) but which nonetheless implies hidden homosexuality as the secret truth. "The Guy Haines of Hitchcock's film certainly does not look homosexual," Corber writes (1993, 70), distancing the character from the actor playing the part, who was gay. Anyone could be gay, whether he looks it or not (whatever "looking it" means). This sameness, to return to Rohmer and Chabrol's point, moots the difference between the wrong man and the right one.

We are everywhere

These questions of sameness and difference open the prospect of a homosexuality without limits. In the only book devoted entirely to the subject of homosexuality and Hitchcock, Theodore Price moves in that direction, but from a homophobic position that needs to be distinguished from the argument I'm making. Building upon the "grand insight"

FIGURE 22. Guy ties Bruno's tie. DVD still.

(1992, ix) of the Rohmer and Chabrol homosexual triptych,
Price finds homosexuality everywhere. Or, rather, as the subtitle of his book announces, Price sees "Jack the Ripper and
the Superbitch Prostitute" as the basic figures in Hitchcock's
films. Homosexuals, for him, fill the Jack the Ripper role. For
Price, at the root of all failed heterosexual relations and all
misogyny there lurks a gay man who hates women—a hatred
caused by the fact that he is impotent with women and "cannot make love to them effectively" (1992, xiii; this is Price's
diagnosis of Bruno [1992, 27]). Price lists the many dysfunc-
tional and unhappy marriages in Hitchcock's oeuvre, only

to blame their failures on homosexuality (1992, 37–40). He exonerates straights from misogyny and feeds the flames of homophobia. Unlike Barton, who sees that homophobia and misogyny often go hand-in-hand, Price links homosexuality and misogyny. However, what we can take from Price is this: that even as he exonerates straights from the crimes he attaches to homosexuals, he keeps suggesting that the straight/gay difference is precarious; for him, every married man is really gay.

Price thus casts Bruno as the "active homosexual" (1992, 22) and Guy as the married "passive homosexual." He knows Bruno is gay because he is "boyish" and "campy," while Guy is "just a bit effeminate" (1992, 23). He knows they are a couple because after Guy slugs Bruno at Senator Morton's house, he ties Bruno's bow tie for him, "the way a wife might help a husband after a spat" (1992, 19). Rohmer and Chabrol had accused same-sex love of being "only an imitation" (1979, 28) of the real thing. Price does too in his active/passive, husband/wife picture of male-male relations. Admitting, for half a sentence, that "not all real-life homosexuals hate women" (1992, 40), he insists that they do in Hitchcock's films, as if this were some kind of truth about all gay men.

Price's book is remarkable for the ways in which, in 1992, it retailed views of homosexuality that were standard before homosexuality was removed from the psychiatric list of mental disorders in 1973. His book would be Hepworth's perfect target. Certainly what Price makes of Rohmer and Chabrol fits Hepworth's condemnation of them. To my mind, however, Price is less true to them than he is to 1950s medical "experts" on homosexuality such as Irving Bieber or Edmund Bergler who wrote article after article, book after book, on the ills of homosexuality. Kenneth Lewes quotes from Bergler's 1956 book, *Homosexuality: Disease or Way of Life*, in a citation that seems apt to put beside Price's analysis of Bruno and Guy (Price's book has, in its subtitle, *A Psychoanalytic View*): "I have no bias against homosexuality... [but] homosexuals are essentially disagreeable people... displaying a mixture of superciliousness, false aggression, and whimpering,... subservient when confronted with a stronger person, merciless when in power, unscrupulous about trampling on a weaker person" (Lewes 1995, 3).

What is nonetheless of some interest in Price's book is the way he handles the question of visibility. Homosexuality, he knows, is never explicit; it is "The Love That Dare Not Speak Its Name" (1992, ix). Price offers a guide to how he exercises gaydar, listing ten bullet points (1992, 41–42). If a Hitchcock film is based on a novel by a gay author, it must be gay; if the actors are known to be gay, then so are their characters. Homosexuality is "obvious" to those who know the code (e.g., effeminacy or boyish immaturity) or "not-so-obvious" until you do (clues: if a man hates a woman, is in a bad marriage, or is passive in relation to women). And the clincher, number ten on the list: you know you are seeing homosexuality on screen if "there are 'bondage' scenes, which often represent a sadomasochistic, master/slave relationship, common to some homosexual relationships" (1992, 42).

All this knowingness about homosexuality as what ruins proper gender relations and heterosexual marriage is deplorable, to be sure. But what is breathtaking about Price's book is that he knows that homosexuality won't be visible on screen as such, and, at the same time, he "knows" it is everywhere. It's for this latter point that, in the course of his often fascinating study of objects, places, and themes in Hitchcock, Michael Walker expresses "sympathy" with Price's project in his chapter on homosexuality. He demurs from Price's assumption that "any sexual reluctance or inhibition on the part of a character ... signals gayness" (2005, 249), but agrees that "homosexual undercurrents are one of the most persistent and significant features to Hitchcock's films" (2005, 52).

Like Hepworth, Walker regards it as "regrettable" (2005, 294) that these undercurrents so often attach themselves to murderous desires, a doubling of forbidden desire and the criminal act of taking a life. Like Hepworth, too, Walker expresses some reservations about the critical stance of Robin Wood, who, according to Hepworth, "neither challenges nor disputes Hitchcock's homophobia" (1995, 190). Whereas Price's project is reckless in the way in which it finds gays to blame everywhere, Walker finds that Wood is "[a] little cautious in his overall estimate of the number of such figures" (2005, 249).

Robin Wood established himself as a major critic of Hitchcock in his 1965 book *Hitchcock's Films*. A dozen or so years later, he came out. In "The Murderous Gays: Hitchcock's Homophobia," reprinted in *Out in Culture*, Wood looks back on his earlier work from this later gay vantage point. If Wood doesn't see homosexuality everywhere in Hitchcock, it's because, he explains, that "prior to the sixties, it was impossible openly to acknowledge even the existence of homosexuality in a Hollywood movie" (1995, 205). Key to his analysis is the concept of repression and the fact of censorship. Since gays can't be out in these films, it prompts Wood to ask a crucial question: "But which, in fact, *are* Hitchcock's gay characters? ... Bruno Anthony in *Strangers on a Train* is supposed to be gay. 'Supposed to be' strikes me as the appropriate way of putting it" (1995, 205–7). That's exactly how it strikes me too. Who supposes, and on what basis? If a man dresses flamboyantly, is he gay? If he kills women, is he gay? If he tells another man he likes him, is he gay? If he seems to have a particularly close relationship to his mother, is he gay? If he is boyish, is he gay? If he has a secret, is he gay? Based on such "evidence," anyone can be "supposed to be." Or not.

"Homosexuality had to be coded, and discreetly," Wood remarks, depending on censorship to explain this. He immediately proceeds much further, however: "[C]oding, even when indiscreet, is notoriously likely to produce ambiguities and uncertainties" (1995, 205). Although Wood believes that censorship and repression explain the ambiguities, his insight suggests a more general point: indirect representation will always leave open the question of deciding whether or not one is seeing homosexuality represented. Or, to put this the other way round: indirect representation is how homosexuality is represented. This is the central point I have been making. It is not just because of the stigmatizing and violent repression of homosexuality, as Wood contends, that homosexuality is unrepresentable. There is no essential truth about homosexuality to be seen.

This is my universalizing, queer assumption; it's not one Wood makes. Recounting his youthful fascination with *Rope* and his inability to see then that his connection with the film was based in his own homosexuality, Wood generalizes. Brandon and Philip, the presumptive lovers in the film, are not allowed to be shown in bed or in embrace (censored); this means they are unable to love because society denies them their love (repressed). From these conditions, Wood almost arrives at the thesis of Rohmer and Chabrol: gay men can't love. He reads the uncorking of a bottle of champagne in *Rope* as an oblique sign that the two men practice solitary "self-masturbation rather than intercourse" (1995, 212). What happened, I have to wonder, to the possibility of ambiguity and uncertainty? How could we be sure they really never do it? "Doubtless in 1948 there were homosexuals who were able to love," Wood writes, but they did so under "almost insuperable ideological odds. For, brought up and conditioned to detest ourselves, how could we love each other—each seeing

FIGURE 23. Callous Bruno bursts the balloon. DVD still.

in the other a reflection and constant reminder of his own sickness and evil?" (Wood 1995, 211).

This is a wrenching statement that no doubt records what being gay felt like to seventeen-year-old Robin Wood. It's an experience that gay youth can have now as well, to be sure. But I don't think that what follows from this is some set of general truths about gay oppression or the work that Hitchcock's films do to replicate, or, worse, encourage and enforce it. So, alongside Wood's account, put what Robert J. Corber tells us at the end of the acknowledgments to his book: "This project began as an attempt to understand the political and sexual taboos of my childhood, which included not being allowed to watch *Strangers on a Train* when it was shown on television because, according to my mother, it was a film about 'homos'" (1993, ix–x). His mother did not say it was a homophobic film, and she clearly did not think seeing it would help her son go straight. Au contraire. Perhaps we could put beside this anecdote a remark Claude Chabrol made in a 2001 interview with Peter Lennon about his decision to become a filmmaker: "My mother explained that the cinema was full of homosexuals. As far as I was concerned, either I was a homosexual or I wasn't, so making films would change nothing."

We're here, we're queer, get used to it!
In his chapter in *No Future* on *The Birds*, with its airborne attack on children that he finds central to the meaning of the film, Lee Edelman pauses over a congruent moment in *Strangers on a Train.* This is the brief scene during Bruno's first trip to the Metcalf Amusement Park when, pursuing Miriam, he is accosted by a small boy in cowboy attire holding a balloon. The boy points his toy gun at Bruno and Bruno "punctures the balloon of cuteness that hangs like a halo above one annoying child" (Edelman 2004, 121).

Bruno exemplifies what Edelman dubs *sinthom*osexuality. The italicized part of the word he takes from Jacques Lacan (and Slavoj Žižek). *Sinthom* comes from an old French form of the word that means "symptom"; the term designates the unsocialized core that defines each person's unconscious desire. Edelman's new word links this core to homosexuality, taking at its word the most homophobic voices in our culture, which endow homosexuality with a culture-destroying power. For Edelman, Bruno is in this world-destroying position when he punctures the halo around the child because in modern western society (perhaps especially in the US), in ideological discourses, the child is invested with the value of saving and preserving culture. "The future rests with our children" is a recurring slogan, and not just that of the conservative right or the Catholic Church.

For Edelman, this fantasy of the child is pernicious. It compels gays who wish to be regarded as participants in the social contract to advocate marriage, child-rearing, and military service as the only ways to prove the legitimacy of our existence. It means that the only way to respond to homophobia is to refuse subversive ways of being gay. It is to seek to be indistinguishable from the heterosexual norms that oppress gays.

Edelman offers a powerful and provocative political position. Even more is at stake for him than politics, however. To subscribe to "reproductive futurism" (2004, 2) is to be in the grips of a massive illusion: the fantasy of life through the child is a way of denying that we die. The fantasy of the child represents a denial that at the core of each of us is an entirely contingent, unsocialized, and determining force. Edelman attaches it to the Freudian death drive: this drive is meaningless, repetitive, incapable of satisfaction. "The drives always seek a form of satisfaction that, from a Freudian or traditional moralistic standpoint, is considered perverse" (2004, 114, quoting Bruce Fink). Society considers homosexuality, Edelman continues, "as a mode of enjoyment at the social order's expense" (ibid.). Edelman urges his readers to assent to this proposition, to take our anti-social, unsocialized pleasures. By agreeing to represent the force that would destroy society, we stand for something in everyone that opposes the narrowing of desire to the norms of heterosexual reproductive culture.

Edelman's arguments are related to a queer position we have seen before, in particular in Sedgwick's parsing of the minoritarian and universalizing claims around homosexuality. At the same time that Edelman seems to support a minoritarian view when he enjoins us to assent to the negative figurations of homosexuality, we serve to illuminate a truth that is not just about homosexuals who refuse the social tasks allied to reproduction. Society would refuse those who do not "fit," as if everyone else does. But were gays to achieve inclusion in society by adopting mainstream lifestyles—a highly contested possibility in the US—that would not end exclusion and stigma, which would still attach to nonconforming gays as well as to the many others rejected by the culture. "No historical category of abjection is ever simply obsolete," Edelman writes (2004, 115). A glance at the profile of the poor and the imprisoned in the US, so many years after

FIGURE 24. Bruno gets his kicks. DVD still.

the passage of Civil Rights legislation and the programs of the Great Society, readily points at those still deemed little more than refuse.

Edelman's thesis has been dubbed "the anti-social hypothesis"; he is not the only queer theorist making these arguments. For example, in the culminating chapter on "The Gay Outlaw," in *Homos*, Leo Bersani asks the provocative question, "Should a homosexual be a good citizen?" (1995, 113). He answers it in the negative. Like Edelman, Bersani attaches citizenship to sexual normativity; for him it lies in a vision of social relations modeled in interpersonal intimacy. Bersani posits a notion of sameness that he calls our homo-ness. He bases it not in the notions of intimacy and otherness that he challenges, but in a sameness that paradoxically would allow for difference, "a community in which relations would no longer be held hostage to demands for intimate knowledge of the other" (1995, 151). We are all the same because we share an existence with and in the world. This "community" does not privilege human difference. It ties us to each other because the world was not made for us, and yet we are all part of it. It refuses the "intimacy" that is inevitably tied to those who society deems worthy of having intimate relations: the heterosexual couple.

Bersani offers a community of non-relationality. It is not hostage to heteronormativity. It can be exemplified in *Strangers on a Train* in another scene that captures Edelman's attention, Bruno on the out-of-control merry-go-round, relentlessly kicking Guy's hand, attempting to throw him off. Edelman recalls this scene in his chapter-long analysis of *North by Northwest*. Its focus is on the moment late in that film when Leonard (Martin Landau) refuses Roger O. Thornhill's (Cary Grant) call for help as he hangs precariously on the edge of Mount Rushmore, holding Eve Kendall (Eva Marie Saint) by one hand, his other grasping the ledge. In response, Leonard, rather than offering help, steps on Thornhill's hand.

In "Hitchcock's Homophobia," Hepworth seized on Leonard's action for his evidence against Hitchcock.

Leonard's actions are "cold-blooded," and "Leonard is a monster," he writes, "*because* he is gay" (1995, 189). Edelman treats the scene as a prime instance of *sinthom*osexuality. Leonard, Edelman writes, is a "victim of compassion's compulsory disavowal of its own intrinsic callousness" (2004, 72). Earlier in the film, US government agents were quite willing to let Thornhill die in order to protect the cover of their double agent, Eve Kendall. Edelman insists that we put Leonard's callous actions beside the government's callousness. In both cases it is a matter of saving Eve Kendall. But, Edelman insists, when Leonard stamps on Thornhill's hand he could be rescuing him from her and, more importantly, from the fantasy of the happy ending and futurity that she represents. Hitchcock goes out of his way to underscore that it is a fantasy when the film cuts abruptly to Thornhill holding his hand out to Eve, no longer on the cliff, but in the upper berth of a train compartment; he addresses her as "Mrs Thornhill." The closing shot of the film shows the train disappearing into a tunnel. Edelman quotes Hitchcock on this conclusion: "It's a phallic symbol. But you mustn't tell anyone" (2004, 98), he says, tongue-in-cheek.

For Hepworth, Leonard is a gay monster who reeks of Hitchcock's homophobia; for Edelman he performs the exemplary act of showing up compassion for what it is: a willingness to lend a helping hand but only when it helps the prevailing social order to believe it is always right, including when it decides who ought to be sacrificed. Since we are the ones likely to be sacrificed, being a monster might well be preferable to being a good citizen.

North by Northwest is further comparable to *Strangers on a Train*. Bruno is every bit as callous as Leonard. He would shake Guy loose from the supposition of their radical difference. Moreover, we might recall that Roger Thornhill first meets Eve Kendall on a train, that space made for chance encounters and anonymous sociality. But like Guy with Bruno, Thornhill may think he is unknown to the stranger on the train, but she in fact knows very well who he is, and not only because his face (like Guy's) has been in the newspaper. Kendall knows who Thornhill is because, as a double agent, she is on the train to seduce him in order to turn him over to her Soviet boss and lover, Phillip Vandamm (James Mason). Vandamm wants him dead because he thinks that Thornhill is a US agent. In fact, in one of those typical Hitchcock wrong-man plots, Thornhill has been mistaken for an agent who does not actually exist. This fictitious figure is a cover invented to protect Kendall, a US agent planted among and sleeping with the enemy. Kendall is seducing Thornhill as much for her US boss (played by Leo G. Carroll, the same actor who plays Senator Morton in *Strangers on a Train*), as for the enemy, Vandamm: both want Thornhill out of the way. There is callousness on both sides, the "right" one and the "wrong" one, and the political game is being played as seduction.

In the scenes on the train in *North by Northwest*—first in

a public space, then in Eve Kendall's compartment (the same rhythm as in *Strangers on a Train*)—Thornhill falls for the double agent. It's easy enough to see that she is being made a misogynist patsy in this convoluted plot. That certainly needs to be registered in an analysis of the film (much the same has to be said about Miriam). But it also is just as easy to see Edelman's point: that the clear demarcations of identity are in question along with the mystification of heterosexual love in this meeting of supposed strangers on a train. So, too, when Bruno and Guy meet. These encounters on the train bear all the signs of the unaccountable, the insistence on a drive that drives people apart even as it seems to bring them together. *Sinthom*osexuality.

In his conversation with Eve Kendall, Thornhill mentions that his middle initial "O." stands for nothing. It is just this meaninglessness that *sinthom*osexuality unveils. Leonard repudiates sociality (he offers no helping hand) and refuses futurity by performing what Edelman terms an "impossible ethical act" (2004, 101) in his lack of compassion. Leonard is like Bersani's gay outlaw who does not want simply to overturn society so much as to refuse it entirely.

Hitchcock's vision of murderous gays, if we want to describe Leonard or Bruno in Robin Wood's terms, encompasses a highly ironic sense of the good that replaces such evil. In the course of *North by Northwest*, Thornhill goes from being an irresponsible playboy who believes in nothing to becoming the devoted lover of a double agent who can

FIGURE 25. Bruno and Guy talk the same talk. DVD still.

make any side believe she is on their side; earnest Thornhill, coming to believe in country, mom, and apple pie, has tuned out the Bruno that Leonard seeks to awaken by stamping on his hand. As Edelman writes, Leonard, when doing so, seems to be channeling Bruno, "as if responding thereby to the earnestness with which Thornhill tunes Bruno out" (2004, 78). That initial Roger Thornhill is as much a *sinthom*osexual as is Leonard at its close. Perhaps double agent Eve Kendall is too.

Leonard's refusal to do what society expects might be put beside the exchange when Guy exits Bruno's compartment. "We do talk the same language," Bruno says to Guy, and Guy agrees, "Sure, we talk the same language." A moment later, Bruno continues, "You think my theory is okay, Guy? You like it?" and again, Guy goes along with him: "Sure, sure, Bruno. They're all okay." Guy, we might want to say, is only humoring Bruno, playing the social game of agreement when he does not mean what he says. As Mladen Dolar comments on this and four similar moments in *Strangers on a Train*, they highlight the way in which "the very form of politeness implies a capacity to read the implications, read between the lines, not to take words at their face value" (1992, 41). This means that the social contract depends as much as the unsocial dissolution of that contract does on a disparity between words and meaning. If this scene of agreement is a tissue of polite lies and does not mean what it says, it points to a realm of meaninglessness that underlies the social contract. It suggests that Guy could as easily mean that he likes Bruno's ideas even if he doesn't think he does.

It is this disparity that the *sinthom*osexual highlights. We can see this, too, in the final encounter on the train. Guy runs away from a minister who has accosted him with the words that Bruno first uttered, identifying him by name. In the course of his reading of *Rope*, and especially of the role that denotation and connotation play in that film, D.A. Miller comments on the "normal-seeming" (1990, 122) nature of this final scene from *Strangers on a Train*. Enacted in the vein of "light comedy," Guy now refuses what he had entertained with "homosexual, homosexualizing Bruno" (ibid.). Miller argues that this final move, with Anne, away from the preacher, does less to establish Guy's heterosexuality as to make it a matter of "*nonhomosexuality*; as such, it is always and only engaged in rejecting a determination that thus can't fail to determine it" (ibid.).

Miller's reading of *Rope* is provoked by the ease with which critics quickly allude to the homosexuality of that film without a shred of evidence beyond innuendo, and dwell compulsively on its technical trick, the illusion that the film is a single shot. He argues that these two critical positions are related. The film, he shows, masks half of its cuts by fading to black on the rear ends of men, while it leaves the other cuts quite visible. In its play of visibility and invisibility, it plays on the desire (a homophobic one, to be sure), to see what the audience does and does not want to see: evidence of gay male sex. The blackened backsides allude to the supposed negativity and nothingness of anal sex, homosexual sex imagined as entirely non-generative and death-delivering.

It's against this kind of supposition that Edelman argues. Straight and gay cannot be so easily distinguished. Everyone has an anus. All sex is not procreative. Identity is not fixed. Queer, as Edelman insists, is the refusal of identity. Hitchcock is attached to the *sinthom*osexual. Edelman recalls how Hitchcock fantasized that *North by Northwest* might usher in a future in which the director would be able to control his audience by pushing buttons attached to electrodes in their brains as they moved from unbearable fear to uncontrollable laughter (2004, 81). In this fantasy, the auteur is hardwired to the viewer's drive, going straight to the perverse core.

Hitchcock gets there through his formalism. Recall that it was the director's meaningless manipulation, his artistry, that led Bosley Crowther to condemn *Strangers on a Train* for its "touches." Just this attention to the film-as-film, to its patterns of straight lines and circles, led Rohmer and Chabrol beyond their homophobic pronouncements to a recognition of a more universal aspect of Hitchcock's films. That universal aspect is the undoing of the social. When Hitchcock's films get to us, that's where they arrive—at a site of disquieting pleasure.

The repressive hypothesis

The anti-social hypothesis in queer theory does not sit well next to the criticism of Hepworth, which deplores Hitchcock's homophobia. Neither Edelman nor Bersani believe that the social acceptance of gays would solve the problem that homophobia exposes. Hepworth and Wood wrangle a bit in the pages of *Out in Culture*, but they in fact agree on one point: that repression of homosexuality is the cause of homophobia. Liberation, they imply, is all it would take to make gays acceptable to mainstream society. "Had Hitchcock actually argued that under certain circumstances and with certain personalities, sexual *repression* can lead to violence, his work would hold up under scrutiny, but he argues emphatically that sexual *perversion* (often gay sexuality per se) can, and seemingly always does, lead to violence," Hepworth writes (1995, 193). In "the Hitchcock psyche," Wood comments, "repressed homosexuality and its inevitable corollary homophobia may form a significant part" (1995, 197). Ostensibly, his films may seek to show "homosexuality as a perversion" but what they reveal is "society's perversion of homosexuality" (1995, 211).

Rather than entertaining this repressive hypothesis, I'd follow Slavoj Žižek, who comments on those uncanny moments when Guy and Bruno seem to think each other's thoughts, or share a frame in which the words of one are superimposed on the image of the other, or when matching shots place them each in the same place. Opposing the critics who read Guy as a repressed homosexual and Bruno as the outer expression of his interiority, Žižek comments: "This 'transference of guilt' does not concern some psychic interior, some repressed, disavowed desire hidden deep beneath the mask of politeness, but quite the contrary, a radically external network of inter-subjective relations" (1991, 74). His mention of "politeness" recalls the exchange between Bruno and Guy when they "speak the same language." It suggests that homosexuality is not the buried secret, but is always available in linguistic connotation. As D.A. Miller insists, there is more to be seen than a world of social conformity in Hitchcock's films.

In his 1965 essay on *Strangers on a Train*, intent upon arguing that Hitchcock was a moralist in favor of an ordered

FIGURE 26. Bruno's unmoving head. DVD still.

society, Wood voiced a version of his later repressive hypothesis as the truth of Hitchcock's films: "[O]rdered life depends on the rigorous and *unnatural* suppression of a powerfully seductive underworld of desire" (2002, 94; his emphasis). The antisocial thesis tells us, rather, that Hitchcock's films put that "underworld" on screen. As Edelman says in an essay on *Rear Window*, whose title he connects to an anal view, Hitchcock shows "what stands behind the Symbolic order" (1999, 91). Edelman's "behind" is a pun. Hitchcock shows us what is excluded from meaning. In *Strangers on a Train*, we can see this best in those shots when Bruno stands utterly still. He is the dark blot on the stairs of the Jefferson Memorial. Even more stunning is his unmoving head in the scene when he sits in the stands watching Guy play a tennis game. In that shot, the heads of the other spectators move back and forth, following the ball in play. It's as if their heads were that ball. They are playthings of the conventions of seeing that the game demands. They are in the throes of something that makes them behave not as humans with their own volition, but more like machines, each identical to each other.

At the center of this moving image, there is the utterly still Bruno. Unmoving, it is as if he is dead. Yet we know from the montage that his gaze is on Guy. His gaze also is on us. He sees us in something of the way in which the camera sees. An eye is upon us that does not seem human. It persists; it does not move. It holds us. This is the kind of seeing through which, Edelman argues, Hitchcock's films see the world, from the inhuman vantage of the death drive. The head-moving humans in this scene are automatons. Bruno is inert and fixed. He is, as it were, what moves them.

The exclusion from meaning is the homophobic burden that the *sinthom*osexual bears. In this scene at the tennis court, Bruno is set apart from the crowd. But the social world is itself a machine, and its strange life/death is imaged in Bruno. From this perspective, any dream of social ameliora-tion must be an illusion. It ignores what drives us apart. We're here, we're queer, but for Edelman and Bersani there is no getting used to it; for them, that's a good thing.

ᏆᏛ

I've concluded this chapter with a rehearsal of these radical theoretical positions, which I find compelling, not least because so much criticism of Hitchcock has been couched in a psychoanalytic vein that assumes the norms of heterosexual difference. Edelman and Bersani, in positing their anti-social views, are questioning heterosexual privilege. But although Bersani posits a shared "homo-ness," he does not mean that everyone "really" is gay. And while Edelman thinks that *sinthom*osexuality is a universal truth, he, too, does not suppose everyone is gay. In declining to essentialize identity even as he universalizes *sinthom*osexuality, Edelman contributes to a central point in queer theory that is crucial, I have been arguing, to our understanding of Hitchcock's *Strangers on a Train* as a queer classic. Queer theory gets us beyond the question of whether either Bruno or Guy, or both of them, really is gay without having to posit the possibility that one or the other is or isn't. From this vantage point, the question of Hitchcock's homophobia ceases to be a central concern, and we can do more than condemn his films.

THREE: *STRANGERS ON A TRAIN* X TWO

"This picture," Truffaut says in conversation with Hitchcock about *Strangers on a Train*, "is systematically built around the figure 'two' ... Whether it's Guy or Bruno, it's obviously a single personality split in two." Hitchcock agrees, chiming in: "That's right. Though Bruno has killed Guy's wife, for Guy it's just as if he had committed the murder himself" (1983, 199). Here Truffaut and Hitchcock exchange views on the theme of the double that has been the subject of much critical commentary on *Strangers on a Train*. Earlier in their interview, a version of the figure two also comes up when Truffaut encourages Hitchcock in his admiration of the opening shots of the film—the feet and the tracks, paralleling and crisscrossing. "Isn't it a fascinating design?" Hitchcock coos in response and self-regard. "One could study it forever" (1983, 195).

In reading *Strangers on a Train* under the figure two in this chapter, I pursue two aspects of the film that I think are central to its queer interest: the doubles in the film and the relationship of the film to Patricia Highsmith's novel. Hitchcock critics have tended to downplay the latter relationship, guided, no doubt, by the fact that the film departs from its literary source in an absolutely crucial respect when it fails to have Guy go through with the bargain struck, however equivocally, upon the train. Donald Spoto, for example, dismisses the novel as a "somewhat breathlessly florid melodrama" (1983, 321), while

Robert Corber excoriates it as "blatantly homophobic" (1993, 69). What Corber sees in Highsmith is not very different from what led John Hepworth to lambaste Hitchcock. Highsmith's novel does not deliver an unequivocally gay Guy or Bruno; gay implications hover around them, but they can scarcely be read as positive role models: both men are murderers. When Spoto labels the novel "florid," he may be coding its sexuality in a somewhat similar way. He complains that the novel lacks the moral order that he and many other critics think gives enduring value to Hitchcock. This opposition to moral order, I would suggest, is a value—a queer value—in Highsmith and Hitchcock.

Robin Wood's 1965 book is a likely reference point for Spoto's "moral" position. Wood constantly plots a world of order against dark forces that need to be faced and overcome. The relationship of Guy and Bruno, for instance, is found disturbing in this way; their relationship is "not quite natural," and what binds them is a "not quite explicable link" (2002, 86). Without exactly saying so, Wood's terms—the unnatural, the inexplicable—point to what I have been arguing in this book, reading the film as a queer project; the novel also is one, but not in exactly the same way, as I suggested in the opening pages of this study. Highsmith paints an antisocial vision that doubles Guy and Bruno; Hitchcock seems to circumscribe her corrosive text when Guy refuses to be drawn into Bruno's web, his plot to exchange murders. This limit may be illusory— the inexplicable and the unnatural are central to Hitchcock's vision. It's why, we may recall, Raymond Chandler had so much trouble providing a screenplay. In Hitchcock's *Strangers on a Train*, doubling never stops. Paradoxically, Guy's refusal to keep the bargain struck on the train, to which I return now, opens the way for Hitchcock's queer project.

Crisscross double-cross

Guy's decision not to kill Bruno's father in the film is anything but forthright. He telephones Bruno to tell him that he has decided to kill his father. This is the only time in the film that Guy calls Bruno; the significance of the call can be read along the lines that Ned Schantz suggests in his remarkable analysis of the technology of the telephone in film. Phoning, Schantz suggests, furthers "the fantasy of limitless self-extension" (2008, 57). The telephone, that is, serves as a site of the telepathy that film itself accomplishes when it covers distance: we've seen this happen when Guy, speaking to Anne on the phone, says he could have strangled Miriam, and Bruno's hands appear on screen.

The telephone call aims to offer the immediate presence of voice to two people at a distance from each other. In the film, Bruno calls Guy twice as one way to continue the face-to-face encounter on the train. Guy first receives a call from him at Southampton; later, Bruno calls him in Senator Morton's office. In the novel, Bruno calls Guy innumerable times. "Every telephone suggested Guy. He could reach Guy now with two well-placed calls... The one thing Bruno needed to

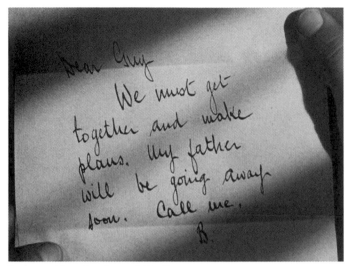

FIGURE 27. A letter from Bruno. DVD still.

make his happiness complete was to hear Guy's voice" (2001, 107). By calling Bruno this one time in the film, Guy seems to agree to his plan. He appears to be reciprocating Bruno's calls, to be effecting the crisscross that Bruno imagined on the train. Seeming to assent to the murder, he is on the verge of becoming Bruno.

Guy proceeds to the Antony mansion, Bruno's gun in hand, and the key that Bruno has sent him providing access; the floor plan, also mailed to him (special delivery), maps his route to Bruno's father's bedroom. Key and floor plan came to Guy through the post, as did a note from Bruno to Guy.

FIGURE 28. Bruno on the phone with Guy. DVD still.

In the novel there are an astonishing number of such letters: Guy tallies the receipt of Bruno's twenty-first (2001, 124), and it is by no means the last one he receives. Indeed, when he goes to murder Bruno's father in the novel, he doesn't need to have Bruno's messages in his hand; Bruno's words are in his head. Letters, an older technology of communication than the phone, have a similar aim: to make another person present across time and space, in script rather than with the immediacy of sound.

In the film, Bruno's communications in writing can appear as magical as telephonic transport. A letter arrives in Guy's apartment with no visible agency to explain its delivery. Locked doors don't keep letters out (or the phone from ringing). Guy is not safe in Senator Morton's office; there he receives a letter as well as a phone call. (Having a key to the Antony residence only points to how much more prosaic Guy's powers are compared to Bruno's.) These technologies of communication suggest vulnerability to penetration. Guy could be taken over by Bruno, could be available to Bruno even when Bruno is at a distance from him. Proceeding to Bruno's family house, Guy seems entirely under his sway, guided by his script. Approaching the door of the bedroom, Guy brandishes Bruno's gun—and then pockets it.

The way Hitchcock frames these scenes does not make the viewer fear for or identify with Bruno's father. The point of view is Guy's. Indeed, Bruno's father barely appears in the film at all (he plays a small part in the novel, too). Bruno crosses his father's path to make his Southampton call to Guy. Guy and Bruno are in the forefront as the film cuts from a shot of Guy in the locker room to Bruno on the phone. In the distance, Mr Antony argues with his wife; we make out a word or two about restraining Bruno and hear Bruno's mother's attempts to get her husband to change his tone with Bruno. Mr Antony is relegated to the background (the shouting bully is as marginalized here as when he becomes the frozen demonic face in Bruno's mother's painting). Hitchcock's film does not love Bruno's father any more than Bruno does. In the long-distance call with Guy, Bruno is visibly and audibly

FIGURE 29. Bruno in bed, waiting for Guy to arrive. DVD still.

closer to Guy than he is to his father in the next room.

In the scene in which Guy is presumably going to kill Bruno's father, Hitchcock generates fear and worry—for Guy, not for Bruno's father. Thus, no sooner is he in the dark and gothic hallway of the house than a huge Great Dane menaces him on the stairway. Then, in a brief, uncanny slow-motion shot, the growling dog proves kind and licks Guy's hand. The viewer is presumably relieved to find that Guy is in no danger. If we are being made complicit with a murderer, we're also being used, double-crossed, as the scene makes clear once Guy enters the bedroom, if not before when he pockets the gun. Murmuring

"Mr Antony," it would not seem likely that Guy has come to kill. Then the lights go on, and Bruno, fully clothed, pops up in bed. (This bit is a contribution of Raymond Chandler's.)

Crisscross has become double-cross, and doubly so: Guy claims never to have intended to kill Bruno's father. Bruno claims that he had no time on the phone to tell Guy that his father was not at home. Suspecting Guy of a double-cross, Bruno is there to double-cross him. Rather than this being a moment of definitive dis-identification—the moment when Guy definitively breaks with Bruno—Guy double-crosses Bruno when Bruno double-crosses him.

What should we make of this scene between Guy and Bruno? In his compelling essay, "Hospitality and the Unsettled Viewer," Ned Schantz offers us five ways we could read the scene (2010, 5). First: We could believe that Guy never intended to kill Bruno's father—although, second: there is plenty of evidence to believe the opposite, that he has come there to kill him; that is, presumably, what we think until the moment of suspense yields to the surprise of finding Bruno in his father's place. We have further reason to believe that Guy really plans to murder Bruno's father when we consider the sequence leading up to his call. Guy telephones Bruno just after Senator Morton's party, the point in the film when, uncannily, Guy feels most cornered by Bruno despite the fact that Bruno has come very close to revealing himself as Miriam's murderer. Anne's question, "How did you get him to do it?" is what the police will think; Anne is now acting as guilty as Guy is, knowing what Bruno did, knowing it will look as if Bruno did what Guy wanted him to do. These worries motivate Guy's visit to the Antony house.

Alongside the mutually exclusive possibilities that Guy has come to kill Bruno's father or to warn him about his son, there's also, Schantz notes (third), the question of the dog: does he lick Guy because he recognizes him? Could it be that Guy has been there before? Is Guy arriving for a lovers' assignation? Whether or not we wonder (as Schantz does) whether Guy has been at Bruno's house before and, if so, has been to bed with him, the threatening dog that turns loving seems like a perfect symbol or image of Bruno—unless, that is, it's the image of what Guy could do to turn Bruno's menacing threats into something else. Finding Bruno in bed certainly lends the scene a sexual implication, although having him clothed seems also to veil that possibility. It's like a moment in a dream when the unconscious will only go so far to allow one what one desires. That desire to be in bed together could be Guy's; it also could be Bruno's. When Bruno turns on the light to reveal himself in bed, he claims he had no time on the phone to stop Guy from coming. Really? The phone call wasn't all that short. Why did Bruno want Guy to find him in bed waiting for him?[11]

Once again, we have two opposing, although not, this time,

---

11. Dyer similarly wonders whether Bruno set Guy up "in the hope of homosexual seduction" (1993, 67).

exclusive possibilities: each may be there to have sex under the pretext of being there to kill. For, after all, the matching murder plot that Bruno proposed on the train was also the way in which the two men bonded. So Schantz proceeds from the sexual possibilities to his remaining (fourth and fifth) speculations: Perhaps Bruno has lured Guy there in order to kill him. Or, lastly, perhaps Guy has gone there to kill Bruno. Why not? Killing and loving don't seem so far apart.

Guy has found himself in the Antony mansion because he has been driven there by Bruno's penetration of the Senator's party and his virtual re-enactment there of Miriam's murder. In the scene that follows, in a parallel move, doubling Guy, Anne pays a visit to the Antony house; Guy doesn't know about this beforehand, just as his visit to Bruno's home was unknown to her. This visit also occurs under the aegis of a bizarre form of hospitality. Mrs Antony treats Anne's visit as a social call and has the ready-made phrases of sociability at hand; "Very nice of you to call," she says to the distraught young woman. So damaged by life in the Antony household, Mrs Antony survives thanks to social convention (and therapeutic painting). "Come see us again sometime" is her parting line to Anne, displaying perfect hostess manners.

The police knew that Guy had given them the slip when they heard his phone ringing for half an hour. Was the caller Anne, trying to reach Guy to figure out what they might do about Bruno? And was Anne's notion that, if she could talk to Bruno's mother, the two women could solve the muddle in

FIGURE 30. Mrs Antony entertains Anne. DVD still.

which the two men found themselves? If so, the film locates the impossibility of this woman-to-woman solution precisely in the socializing of women that (within a patriarchy) makes them subordinate to men. Like mother, like son: Mrs Antony's way of dealing with her husband is to cling to the son who loves her and is so like her. The scene between Anne and Mrs Antony moves to become the sadistic scene between Bruno and Anne that Hepworth deplored. But perhaps just as sadistic—and directed at the two women—is the scene of impossible female bonding. It is, in fact, against a suppressed backdrop of female-female communication and bonding that

Schantz reads the letters in novels and the telephones in films, on the lookout for the world of gossip that might make possible a world of women without men. In the scene between Anne and Bruno's mother, Hitchcock holds out (even as he makes impossible) this alternative to the intense male bonding in the film.

There is nothing like this woman-to-woman scene in Highsmith's novel. In part, this is because lesbian Highsmith has no sympathy for women ruined by patriarchy. At the plot level, there is no occasion for Anne and Mrs Antony to get together in the novel because Guy goes through with the murder of Bruno's father. In the film, Guy goes to the Antony mansion to try to stop a plot that involves Anne; this is also his motive for killing Bruno's father in the novel—to keep Bruno away from Anne (Bruno has already sent her an anonymous letter implicating Guy in the murder of Miriam).

To keep Anne from being drawn into Bruno's plot is not the entire reason Guy decides to kill Bruno's father in the novel, for his love for her diminishes as he becomes more and more enmeshed with Bruno. In the modality that characterizes his doubling relationship with Bruno in the novel, Guy commits the murder for two opposing reasons. On the one hand, he murders Bruno's father to fulfill the bargain and thus "rid himself of Bruno" (Highsmith 2001, 140). On the other hand, he commits the murder to cement his relationship with Bruno: "He was like Bruno ... Hadn't he known Bruno was like himself? ... He loved Bruno" (2001, 148). These conflicting thoughts occur just pages apart. In between, as happens often in the novel, Guy imagines Bruno is there with him. This time—and it's not the only time such premonitions, such dreaded desires are realized—he wakes to find it true. The proximity that technology promises is uncannily manifest when Bruno appears in Guy's bedroom. "He was quite happy that Bruno had come ... 'Hi,' Bruno said softly ... 'You're ready now, aren't you?'" (2001, 144).

Although Guy's betrayal of Bruno in the film is not the end of their relationship, the scene between Guy and Bruno in the Antony house does provide a last word for it. Telling Guy that he won't shoot him in the back as Guy descends the stairs, Bruno assures him that he's "a very clever fellow" and will figure out a better way to deal with him. After Bruno dies, the man who identified him as Miriam's murderer, and thus helped save Guy from the police, asks Guy who Bruno was: "Bruno, Bruno Antony," Guy says, "a very clever fellow." Bruno writes his own epitaph on the stairs when Guy turns his back on him; Guy repeats his words. The stage direction in a December 12, 1950 script in the Warner Bros. Archives indicates that Guy says these lines "reminiscently and a little compassionately, remembering what Bruno had said of himself" (155). However much the film has drawn them apart, it is nonetheless the case that Guy's last words about Bruno are Bruno's words about himself. He has, in that way, become Bruno even when separated from him by death.

Since Guy goes through with the murder of Bruno's father

in the novel, one might assume that they remain an insepa-rable pair. However, Bruno dies in a boating accident (it may be a suicide) toward the end of the book. Without "his friend, his brother" (2001, 263), Guy is distraught. Finding his guilt for Miriam's death insupportable without Bruno to share it, Guy seeks to make amends. But who could possibly care that Miriam is dead, he wonders. Only one person must mourn her loss, he thinks: the man who got her pregnant and would have married her if he could. Guy flies to Houston to find Miriam's lover—his name is Owen Markham—in order to confess to him. (Highsmith's Metcalf is a town in Texas; the locale reflects where she came from and marks her identifi-cation with Guy.)

Guy locates Markham and takes him to his hotel room. But, as he unravels his story, he discovers that Markham didn't intend to marry Miriam: "Hell, I didn't love her … I was glad enough not to have to marry her" (2001, 272). The fact that Guy was responsible for her murder by telling Bruno about her does not faze Owen in the least. Desperate for Owen Markham's absolution, Guy tells him that he murdered Bruno's father. Finding that he's talking to a murderer doesn't bother Markham either. "Live and let live" (2001, 277), he says. His impercipient use of clichéd language is his way of saying: kill whomever you want, it doesn't matter to me. "What busi-ness is it of mine?" he asks (ibid.).

Owen's indifference prompts Guy to respond by saying "it's society's business," and then to reflect on his own clichéd answer. What could "society" mean if no one cares about the death of Miriam—or about Bruno's father either, it would seem. Guy's thoughts lead him to Highsmith's version of the anti-social hypothesis, to her version of the statement Bruno makes in the film: "What's a life or two, Guy? Some people are better off dead." Life has no sacred meaning. For Highsmith's characters, murder is a way of making meaning, a way of proving that one is not bound by a baseless conventional morality.

In the novel, Bruno speaks a line on the train that did not survive into the final cut of the film: "Any kind of person can murder" (2001, 29). As Kristen Hatch has suggested, the line about murder seems to be the equivalent of the universalizing notion about sexuality that was being propounded about the time. "When Bruno announces to Guy that he believes that anyone is capable of murder his words echo Alfred Kinsey's conclusion that anyone is capable of homosexual desire" (2005, 55). This equation folds into the antisocial thesis in Highsmith: the conventional rules of society bear no relationship to actual people. "The law was not society," Guy thinks (2001, 278). The law imposes morality as a means of social control on the uncontrollable perverse core. The hollowness of morality is exposed when it extends from the condemnation of murder to the condemnation of other crimes—homosexuality, for instance.

"Nobody knows what a murderer looks like," Guy tells Owen, "[a] murderer looks like anybody" (2001, 274)—which could as easily apply to how anyone knows someone is gay.

Guy wonders for a moment whether his conversation with Owen will replicate the conversation he had with Bruno. Is stupid Owen capable of being another Guy to Guy in the role of Bruno? Maybe. However, rather than showing us a world where anyone can murder, Highsmith's novel offers us one where only Guy and Bruno do. In that way, it subscribes to a minoritarian logic, to a logic of exceptionality rather than commonality. Bruno, in fact, says, "Guy and I are supermen" (2001, 261). In the novel, Guy is an architect who dreams of making "perfect" buildings (2001, 100–01); Bruno dreams of committing the "perfect" murder (2001, 34, 106). These are the forms of world-making and world-destroying that Highsmith offers as counters to conventional morality. As an artist, Guy can be brought into the orbit of Oscar Wilde's aesthetics, its refusal of social conventions by those society itself refuses. In her later Ripley novels, Highsmith develops this point. Ripley is an aesthete, a murderer who plays the harpsichord. He is involved with artistic forgery that can't be distinguished from the real thing. The artist is a forger. Ripley succeeds in the world (he lives a life of comfortable bourgeois luxury) even as murder is one means to this end.

It's obvious, too, that Guy and Bruno dabble in the Nietzschean beliefs that characterize the protagonists in *Rope*, where, as Thomas Elsaesser argues, aesthetic outrage joins hands with moral trespass. I've wondered whether Hitchcock was drawn to Highsmith's novel because it owes something to Hitchcock's earlier film and, if so, whether in turning her first novel into his film, Hitchcock wasn't himself caught in a loop of representational doubling. At the very least, the case of Leopold and Loeb lies behind both Hitchcock's *Rope* and Highsmith's novel.

In Hitchcock's film, Guy emerges technically innocent at the end; in the novel, he is not and is caught by the one person who does in fact care about the murders, a private detective formerly employed by Bruno's father. The detective overhears Guy's confession to Owen Markham thanks to a phone he has taken off its receiver. Telephonic penetration has occurred. Guy ends the novel succumbing to the detective in words that suggest an erotic embrace: "Take me," he says (2001, 281). The law becomes a scene of homoerotic desire; Guy's final words seem like something we might find in Genet. Hitchcock, obviously, does not go this far, but certainly Guy's final innocence in the film is very compromised. Guy is no superman, no artist; he's just a tennis player who wants to be a politician. He's anyone, and queer. Hitchcock's version of the antisocial thesis may not be as radical as Highsmith's insofar as murdering stops with Bruno, but it's by no means simply a conservative embrace of law and order either. Whereas Highsmith pins her antisociality onto two exceptional men, Hitchcock suggest that the connection to Bruno may have no limits. Whereas Highsmith has the murder pact fulfilled, Hitchcock leaves it inexplicitly open and, at the same time, pins it, as I will suggest below, to objects whose circulation implicates the ordinary everyday world.

Between men: The cigarette lighter

Highsmith's *Strangers on a Train* begins on the train and proceeds in its opening chapters, much as the film does, in the club car meeting and conversation in Bruno's compartment. Memorable lines come from the novel: " 'I'm a bum' ... 'Who said you were' ... 'My father' " (2001, 17); "I got a theory a person ought to do everything it's possible to do" (2001, 21); "Which do you want, the busted light socket in the bathroom or the carbon monoxide garage" (2001, 33). The basic plot is the same: "We murder for each other, see? I kill your wife and you kill my father" (2001, 34). Bruno's purring "I like you, Guy," is reiterated (2001, 29, 31), even reciprocated in the novel: " 'I like you, too,' said Guy" (2001, 31). The meeting in the novel differs from the film in several crucial ways, however. For one thing, it's told almost entirely from Guy's point of view and lacks the symmetry of shot-reverse-shot that Hitchcock uses as he continues his plotting of doubling parallels begun in the opening sequence of feet. In both film and novel, it is Guy who taps Bruno's foot. In the novel, this is congruent with the fact that Bruno is the object of Guy's fascination—and repulsion (Bruno sports an enormous pimple that compels Guy's revolted gaze). In the film, the tap of the foot appears more accidental.[12]

---

12. Toles notes this and nicely connects it to Guy's leaving the lighter behind (2009, 114), but from it he builds invidious moralistic distinctions—that one hoped would not survive past Rohmer and Chabrol—between childish Bruno and Guy as a socialized figure who becomes "grown-up" and capable of working past his guilty accidental associations (2009, 137).

Although there is much said about Miriam in the novel, Anne, who is on Guy's mind from its opening page, is never mentioned. Guy's failure to mention her motivates Bruno to insist that Guy kill his father—he feels betrayed by Guy's reticence on the train. Bruno supposes that by murdering for Guy, he was establishing a relationship with him, not making it easier for Guy to have Anne. The scene on the train in the novel is, in that respect, so close to being a pick-up that Guy refuses Bruno in just those terms: "Pick up somebody else" (2001, 31), he says. Characteristic of his fully ambivalent response to Bruno, Guy rebuffs Bruno just two lines down from saying that he likes him. What (who) does Guy want?

In the film, Anne immediately comes up in conversation because of the cigarette lighter. There is no lighter in the novel. There, Guy leaves his copy of Plato's *Phaedrus* behind with Bruno, who intends but forgets to mail it back to him. (The detective who finally apprehends Guy finds the lost book; it helps provide him with evidence that Guy and Bruno were on the train together, and thus helps him figure out the plot hatched there.) *Phaedrus* contains the famous allegory of the two horses that represent people's dual nature—reason and passion in conflict. (Do these get visualized on the merry-go-round?) It's an allegory that fits Guy and Bruno and it plays into the theory of the double that gets articulated explicitly much later in the novel. The cigarette lighter, found only in the film, is crucial to it, as Slavoj Žižek insists: "[I]n *Strangers on a Train* the murderous pact between Bruno and Guy holds only so far as the object (the cigarette lighter) is circulating between them" (1989, 183). The lighter is further significant, Žižek suggests, because of its singularity. It countervails the panoply of doubles in the film. It is not just a sign of the relationship between Guy and Bruno, not simply a symbol; their relationship is embodied in it, in a real, material thing.

Unique as it is as an object, I think we can compare the role the lighter plays to the phone calls and letters that move between Bruno and Guy in the film, uncannily bringing them together. The inscription on it, "A to G," is a minimal formula of written communication. Like the letters and phone calls, the lighter overcomes distance and separation. To have Guy's lighter ultimately becomes a way to have Guy.

The moment the lighter is offered to Bruno by Guy, the sequence of shot/reverse shots is replaced with a close-up of the lighter in Bruno's hand. The lighter takes a star turn and the symmetry of matching shots is broken.

Bruno comments on the object, finding the lighter "elegant" (like high-class Anne), but there is more to be said than that. "A to G" may be translated as "Anne to Guy," but not without filling in the blanks. One way to do that would be to read the alphabetical inscription in the lower right of the lighter against and alongside the image of crossed rackets on the upper left. The lighter can be read as a message from Anne to Guy. As Michael Walker suggests, "Anne is signalling what she finds particularly attractive about him," that is, his athleticism (2005, 27). The crossed rackets suggest, moreover, that

FIGURE 31. The lighter's first close-up. DVD still.

she wants to play doubles with him. (Enforcing this visual pun, Bruno orders a pair of doubles from the waiter at the moment he handles the lighter; he notes the pun that he's just made). There is perhaps a further double entendre in Anne's message: the rackets cross, after all. They anticipate the "crisscross" Bruno will utter when the lighter is his.

Crossing is enacted as the lighter moves from Guy to Bruno. From A to G, and then from G to A, from Guy to [Bruno] Antony. "A" does not only mean Anne.[13] Hitchcock,

---

13. For alphabetical speculations along these lines, see Corber (1993, 73) and Barton (1993, 237).

we might recall, has reversed the name of Highsmith's character (he is called Charles Anthony Bruno in the novel). The names Ant[h]ony and Bruno change places; Antony is in the place of Anne when the lighter moves.[14] This singular object between men conveys doubly: it carries Anne's heterosexual desire; it carries Guy's homosexual desire. One desire may replace the other, or, just as likely, they double each other. They might not be so easily distinguished. In the circuit of the lighter, sexuality is queered and passes beyond the absolute difference of gay and straight. The lighter is, at once, the vehicle and the object of a double and queered desire. Did the lighter intimate a double queer desire from the moment "A" was inscribed? Could "A" perhaps mean "anyone," as in "anyone can murder"?

Highsmith invites us to entertain similar thoughts when she has Bruno make the same point about Guy's name: "I meet a lot of guys—no pun—but not many like you," Bruno says (2001, 31). Guy's name is a guy's name. Insofar as "A" can mean Anne or Antony, we find ourselves once again circling around the question of sexual identity, moving between the poles of universalism and minority identity. Gay and straight difference is not stabilized in the emblem on the lighter,

---

14. In all the treatments and scripts, Bruno's last name is spelled Antony; however, in occasional press releases from Warner Bros., Anthony is also sometimes used, and the opening credits do not give the names of characters. I've followed the script spelling. British pronunciation makes no difference between the two possible spellings of the name.

either. Anne may want to play doubles with Guy, but the two rackets are not differentiated sexually; the only difference between them is where they are placed, one to the right, the other on the left, and the oblique angle with which they cross. The rackets reiterate the shots of feet and of the crossing tracks with which the film opened. Anne offers herself as Guy's double. But is Guy's desire only for her?

What should be made of the fact that Anne gave a lighter to a man who says to Bruno that he doesn't smoke much?

Through the rackets, Anne identifies Guy as a tennis player, but Guy plays tennis only as a means to another end, a career in politics. Marrying Anne (the boss's daughter) is a version of the same plot. When she binds their desire in the crossed rackets, is she acknowledging her role in this scenario or not? And when Guy leaves the lighter with Bruno, is he leaving Anne behind? That's what Robin Wood suggests: "He is leaving in Bruno's keeping his link with Ann [sic], his possibility of climbing into the ordered existence to which he aspires" (2002, 87). Guy transfers his affection from elegant Anne to elegant Bruno. Later, in Bruno's compartment, the camera again focuses on the lighter on the table between the men. Only Bruno uses it; and as the scene closes, he fondles it, taps it lightly, looks at it, and sighs, "Crisscross." Whether or not he has read the transfer of Guy's affection in the movement of the lighter into his hands, his "crisscross" more or less says it.

Crisscross is what the lighter said, too. The lighter has moved from "A" to "G," from "G" to "A." Giving Bruno the

FIGURE 32. Guy's shoe cruises Bruno's. DVD still.

lighter perhaps doubles its initial movement from Anne. The second "A," Antony, is, after all, in gender more like Guy than Anne: both are male. Anne wants to play doubles with Guy, but Bruno fits the position better; Bruno is Guy's double, his mirror. Where the lighter goes, Guy's foot had gone before when he "accidentally" tapped Bruno's foot. That was the first time that the opening sequence of parallel shots was broken, for Bruno does not tap back, the two feet don't swing and meet each other. (Unlike the storyboard image published in *Life* on July 9, 1951, where the two feet are heading toward each other [72].) Guy's first "accident," when he taps Bruno's foot (and activates him?), is matched by this second one, when he leaves the lighter behind. Freud tells us that there are no accidents. This is not simply a statement about the unconscious. It's materialized in the lighter. The physical touch of foot to foot (the sign that men use in tea rooms to initiate sex) is now embodied in the lighter that Bruno holds in his hand.

The next time we see the lighter in the film, Bruno is using it to light Miriam's face just before he strangles her. He is seeing her with and in Guy's "light." In the novel, Bruno thinks constantly about Guy as he tries to locate Miriam; he finds her by thinking Guy's thoughts. This thought process is materialized in the film in the lighter. "Is your name Miriam?" he asks, and finding her, he has her by the throat. As Walker comments, the lighter ties together the plots of the film, the plot of desire and the plot of murder: "The lighter does not function simply as a love token, but also connects Guy and Bruno as accomplices in Miriam's murder" (2005, 27). Bruno drops the lighter as he strangles Miriam and then retrieves it. From that moment on, the lighter is on his mind. He mentions dropping it in the scene when he hands Guy Miriam's eyeglasses: had he left the lighter behind, he would have left evidence that Guy had been there. The lighter *is* Guy, and Bruno has him/it.

Bruno mentions the lighter again when he talks to Anne; he tells her that Guy wants him to return to the murder scene to pick up the lighter, which was left there. And in the next scene, as Guy and Anne talk about her meeting with Bruno,

FIGURE 33. Is your name Miriam? DVD still.

Guy knows what Bruno intends to do; because Bruno has said that Guy wants him to retrieve the lighter, he means he is going to leave it there. Guy knows that to read Bruno's meaning, he must read what he says backwards. Crisscross. Mirror images.

The last crisscross involving the lighter is the sequence in which we cut back and forth from the Forest Hills tennis match. Bruno's reach into the sewer, as his hand goes deeper and deeper into this dark and dirty place, extending itself remarkably, might be read as a scene of anal penetration. His fingers touch, drop, but then stroke the lighter (as he had

FIGURE 34. Bruno fists the lighter. DVD still.

FIGURE 35. Bruno lets the lighter go. DVD still.

before in his train compartment when Guy left it with him) before he closes his fist upon it.

In the last shot of the lighter in the film, it is in Bruno's hand. Unclenching its grasp, dead Bruno delivers it, not to Guy but to the police. The circuit is not closed, the lighter does not return to Guy's safekeeping. The lighter can continue to do what Mladen Dolar suggests its function is: it "holds the couple together and disrupts it at the same time" (1992, 39). Insofar as the lighter is like a letter sent from Anne to Guy, from Guy to Bruno, it does not return to either sender. In this way, leaving open what is to follow, queer possibility is maintained all the way to the end of the film, with Guy and Anne avoiding the clergyman on the train, a replay of the initial meeting of strangers on a train. What Bruno unleashed cannot be stopped.

For Žižek, it is important that there be just one lighter, a singular object that houses and conveys the desire that runs between Guy and Bruno. Just as he insists that we not read one character as the unconscious of the other one, and instead see their desires manifested in their action, so, too, the lighter is not merely a symbol but the actual object that runs between them; it materializes what they are doing with each other, how they have each other, exchange places with each other, become each other. We could link the lighter, I think, to another such object that also comes into view at just about the same time that the lighter does, and which similarly engages the camera's close-up lens: Bruno's tie clip with his name emblazoned on it.

Hitchcock follows Highsmith here: her Bruno wears a tie clip with the initials CAB on it; Hitchcock reverses first and last name, arsy-versy, and transfers the alphabetic play to the lighter. With his name blazoned on him, Bruno is anything but a figure of subliminal subterfuge. No hiding or double entendre there. In the scene in the National Gallery of Art, Bruno complains that Guy is making him "come out" in the open; the camera zooms onto the tie clip, following Anne's gaze. Again, when he is entertaining the Dorvilles at the tennis club, Anne's focus is on the tie clip. She is beginning to piece together Bruno's appearances, beginning to see what is manifest: there is more to Bruno and to his relationship with Guy than Guy has admitted. As the October 18, 1950 final script puts it: "She is looking at Bruno, wondering what mystery lies behind this strange individual and why he and Guy have disclaimed any previous acquaintance" (79). What do they have to hide? Their lovers' pact? Their murder plot?

FIGURE 36. Bruno's tie clip first seen. DVD still.

Doubles: Spectacles

"Say, isn't your name Miriam?" (Highsmith 2001, 80). As Jim Clark demonstrates in his blog, when he juxtaposes lines from the novel with those from the film, the murder of Miriam offers "a rare moment of similarity" between the two (Clark 2002). There is a merry-go-round in both, for example, and it is even playing "The Band Played On" in Highsmith as it is in the film. There too, Bruno joins Miriam and her companions to sing along (2001, 78); he follows them to the island, "a neckers' paradise" (2001, 79), and, enacting Highsmith's pun, his hands go round her throat. "His body seemed to harden like a rock... With a leg behind her, he wrenched her backward, and they fell to the ground together with no sound but of a brush of leaves. He sunk his fingers deeper, enduring the distasteful pressure of her body under his... All the power in him he poured out through his hands... He heard himself whimper. She was still and limp now" (2001, 81). Highsmith sexualizes the scene of the murder in this description; Bruno's violence and disgust are palpable, but so, too, is the final quietus, his and hers.

The equivalent in the film is, of course, its most famous shot: the reflection in Miriam's eyeglasses of the scene of her strangulation. "The shot is one of the cinema's most powerful images of perverted sexuality," Wood comments (2002, 90), and most viewers, I imagine, would agree (Clark cites Wood, for instance). Manny Farber, we might recall, remarks how sexual violence is aestheticized in this shot. Indeed, I think that's part of what makes the scene perverse, although in quite a different way from Highsmith's writing of the murder as if it were a scene of rape. The bodies become indistinct in the distorting lens. As they fall, they lose recognizable shape. Bruno's hands, as many have noticed, look like the claw of the lobster that decorated the tie he wore in the opening scene on the train. Visually, he's becoming a cold-blooded crustacean, a *sinthom*osexual. In the glasses, human bodies stop looking human; they become forms, inhuman shapes. The human is being perverted. What it means to be human is called into question. (That was the case as well when Bruno's head

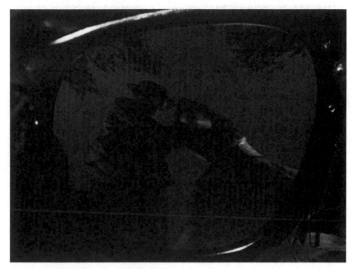

FIGURE 37. The glasses shot. DVD still.

became immobile at the tennis court.) Aesthetization, in its distance from a recognizable representation of the human, brings out the non-human.

The inhuman perverse takes the form here of eyeglasses. Hitchcock gives these to Miriam—they are not in Highsmith's novel—and they become her identifying mark. (Anne will ask Guy about them just at the moment she comes to understand the plot.) When we see Miriam's murder through her glasses, we are seeing it as she sees it. What makes it possible for her to see has been detached from her. If human forms become inhuman in the glasses, Miriam becomes an object through them as well. She can go on seeing, as it were, even when the glasses are lying in the grass. The glasses that see are like Bruno's fixed gaze.

Miriam is not the only woman in a Hitchcock film to wear glasses, and these women function in his work as figures for the women who know too much, to recall the title of Tania Modleski's important book on the viewpoint they represent. These are not the women who, within the normative structures of male/female relationships, exist to be looked at, the women that Laura Mulvey long ago identified as crucial to the syntax of Hollywood films, Hitchcock's centrally among them. These are, rather, women who look. They tend, in Hitchcock films, not to be objects of men's desire, and tend to be paired with and to double women who are the objects of the male gaze (often, Hitchcock's blondes). The women who incite desire don't seem to desire; the women who don't incite desire, do. Miriam provides a kind of crisscross to this dichotomy; she is a site of desire and of repudiated desire, the woman Guy once loved and now loathes, the woman who, however she first felt about Guy, now wants him only to frustrate his desires. Bruno sees her the way Guy does; in his disgusted desire when he strangles her, he assumes Guy's position.

In the film, unlike the novel, Miriam knows Bruno is after her; they exchange glances filled with sexual energy all the way up to the scene of her murder when Bruno lights up her glasses.

Hitchcock's women who know too much are women who can't be controlled by men. They know, moreover, that desire is not in one's own control. Hitchcock's films register this by locating desire outside the person, transferring it from person to person. That it's not one's own desire we've already seen with the cigarette lighter. The eyeglasses present us with another example of this disembodied desire, one lodged in the object, not the person. For Žižek (1992, 125–28), these objects are what he calls, after Lacan, Hitchcock's *sinthoms*. We've encountered Lee Edelman's further development of this concept into *sinthom*osexuality. The objects that convey desire in *Strangers on a Train* are understandable through these concepts insofar as they are vehicles for perverse, non-normative desires. The objects themselves seem trivial and limited in meaning and function—cigarette lighters light cigarettes, glasses help us see. In the film, they are not limited to such denotations, however, but reek of connotation. When Bruno refuses to allow a stranger he meets on the train to use Guy's lighter, it's a clear sign that the lighter is not just a lighter; his struggle to retrieve it from the sewer provokes comment on how attached he is to it, whatever it is.

These objects are akin to Hitchcock's much-remarked MacGuffins, seemingly meaningless items which are at the core of his films. This meaningless core, in psychoanalytic terms, is a way to name the spot of one's own desire, the core of one's own pleasure. It's not the case that we know what that is—it's unconscious. But it knows us. These things are in us and yet outside us. They exist in the strange inside/ outside spaces like those through which characters pass in *Strangers on a Train*: the telephone booth where one is seen to talk, yet not heard; the listening booths in the record shop where Miriam works, which have the same effect; or Bruno's compartment on the train, with its large picture window, as if there might be an audience on the other side of it, who would see the scene whizz by and not hear a word of it. In the compartment, an unspoken conversation takes place through the cigarette lighter.

These objects seem to have minds of their own, or seem to have in mind what the characters cannot know about themselves even as they act in accord with the objects. These objects reveal what we do without our being conscious of what we are doing. As when we are drawn, without knowing why, by a look. As when we somehow forget something very valuable and leave it with someone we think we are happily rid of. As when we insist on something, and then our hand opens involuntarily to tell a truth that contradicts what we were saying. Bruno's dead hand gives him away. In the reflection in Miriam's eyeglasses, Bruno's hand becomes a claw. In the sewer, it seems to have a life of its own.

And, of course, it's not just Miriam's eyeglasses that affect Bruno—it's eyeglasses, period. Bruno hands Miriam's glasses to Guy, but he does not give him back his lighter. Glasses and lighter lie side by side in the strangulation scene. They are paired there, which suggests the similarity between them.

FIGURE 38. Eyeglasses and lighter lie side-by-side. DVD still.

But then they are separated as if, by handing the glasses to Guy, Guy is now free to pursue Anne. But how free is he, when tied to Bruno through the lighter?

Nor is Bruno free of Miriam when he gives her glasses to Guy. She haunts him in the form of eyeglasses. When he meets Anne's sister Barbara, her glasses produce an immediate effect upon him; he sees reflected in them the scene in which he strangled Miriam. "The Band Plays On" plays again; the lighter is mirrored in Barbara's glasses; the voiceover of Bruno asking "Is your name Miriam?" is the question he asks Barbara even though she does not hear the voiceover.

She gets the message the second time this happens, when her glasses trigger Bruno's trance and he is about to re-enact the murder of Miriam using Mrs Cunningham's neck. After the scene clears, Barbara remains, standing transfixed where she stood when Bruno was transfixed looking at her. Like Bruno motionless on the steps of the Jefferson Memorial or at the tennis game, rigidly staring, Barbara doesn't move. Bent over, her arms hanging in front of her, she looks much the way Bruno does in Miriam's glasses. Anne will soon put two and two together and realize that Barbara looks something like Miriam.[15]

Miriam and Barbara don't really look alike except insofar as they both wear glasses, but both produce the same effect on Bruno. Like Miriam, Barbara is a desiring subject; she finds Bruno an interesting-looking Frenchman at first glance. She flirts with Hennessey; deliberately spilling powder on his pants as a subterfuge gives her the opportunity to bend down at his crotch to wipe them clean. It's Barbara who voices the romantic line about how wonderful it would be to have a man love you so much he would kill for you, a line rendered perverse insofar as Bruno comes closest to satisfying it when he kills Miriam so that he can have Guy. In the murder itself, hatred and desire seem perversely the same. "Anne, he was looking at her, but he was strangling me," Barbara says; the

---

15. As one of Hitchcock's "daughters," Modleski cherishes this woman-to-woman moment (2005, 122).

FIGURE 39. Unmoving Barbara. DVD still.

vicarious experience is not much different from the real one. And strangling is, as Highsmith suggested, another form of necking.

If Barbara is another Miriam, as Anne's kid sister she also provides Anne with a double. Anne is remote and controlled; Barbara wears glasses and chases men. But are these doubles so different? When Anne declares her love for Guy and kisses him, he calls her a brazen woman, linking her with Miriam. Barbara's line about how it would be wonderful to have a man love you so much he'd kill for you begins, "I still say." Is this just a persistent romantic notion, or is she reiterating what she said during the conversation that we must imagine to have occurred before Guy arrived at Senator Morton's to hear the news about Miriam? Anne and Barbara must have been discussing the possibility that Guy is responsible for Miriam's death. Anne, after all, heard the proof from his mouth, when he said on the phone that he could strangle her. Anne keeps Guy from saying it again by kissing him. Guy's unspeakable desire—one of them, at any rate—remains unsaid.

Doubles: Pats

To reiterate: "This picture is systematically built around the figure two" (Truffaut 1983, 199):[16]

To begin a list:

two taxis

two pairs of feet

two suitcases

two tennis rackets

two tracks

tennis doubles

double scotches, a pair

two imposters

two boys with Miriam

two children at the fair (one shoots at Bruno; he would toss the other one off the merry-go-round)

two rides on the merry-go-round

---

16. For similar lists, see Spoto (1976, 212–14) and (1983, 327–28), as well as Krohn (2000, 119–24).

two old men (one is shot by one of two cops and the merry-go-
round goes berserk; the other old man stops it when one cop
stops the other from intervening)

Mrs Cunningham and Mrs Anderson (these two also double
Bruno's mother and encourage him, as she does, in parlor
games that turn nasty; the older woman whose car is
commandeered by the cops is akin to these women)

Captain Turley and Sergeant Campbell

Hennessey and Hammond (they have a lovely balletic moment
in Penn Station, cupping their hands over their cigarettes,
turning toward each other; other times they play good-cop/
bad-cop; sometimes they are just a tag team)

two redcaps (railroad employees who carry luggage for
passengers)

two black butlers at Senator Morton's party

two black waiters on the train (and a third tending bar in the
club car; representation of the working class is largely white;
the film is replete with all but invisible servants, bringing
phones on to the scene, opening doors, delivering food,
running concessions at the fair, making the lives of the
protagonists possible)

two fathers

two wives, Miriam and Anne

two sisters, Anne and Barbara

Miriam and Barbara (girls with glasses)

Guy and Bruno

Alfred Hitchcock and his double bass, crossing paths with Guy—
he ascends, Guy descends...

"Isn't it a fascinating design? One could study it forever" (Truffaut 1983, 195).[17] A list of matching shots in the film would be a shot-by-shot account.

Why all these doubles? Spoto gets it half right: "All this doubling...has no precedent in the novel" (1983, 328). The novel does have a theory of doubling; indeed, Bruno tells Anne that it's Guy's constant topic: "what Guy always says, about the doubleness of everything" (2001, 251). (At this late point in the novel, Bruno seems bent on taking Anne away from Guy, either by seducing her, or by strangling her.) "'People, feelings, everything! Double! Two people in each person. There's also a person exactly the opposite of you, like the unseen part of you, somewhere in the world, and he waits in ambush.' It thrilled him to say Guy's words" (2001, 251). Bruno claims to be quoting Guy, but he isn't; yet he isn't exactly putting words into his mouth either. He's Guy's uncanny double in much the way the theory of the double suggests. For it multiplies its notion of doubling: the double could be someone else, a person who exactly replicates oneself. That person, however, could as easily be a part of oneself, the part not seen. Either way, oneself is a misnomer. Either there is someone else out there who is indistinguishable from oneself or one is already divided and doubled.

Although the theory of the double presented in the novel is

---

17. Miller (2010) suggests that such studying, especially when it involves meaningless touches, is how Hitchcock touches the viewer's perverse desire.

FIGURE 40. Hennessey and Hammond arm in arm. DVD still.

a general one about "everything" and everyone, in the novel only Guy and Bruno have this uncanny relationship. The novel, however, suggests that were its doubling proposition true, no one would be safe. Everyone could be menaced by another self. Anyone could be anyone else. There would be no boundaries. There could be no such thing as an individual, the unit upon which social existence depends. Instead of persons, we would have a world of Bersani's "homos," none answerable to a law that assumes individual responsibility and guilt. This is the view that Guy finally articulates in the novel when he realizes that society is a fiction and the law a bugaboo meant to scare people from doing what they want. But what they want, we have seen, is something in them but not them, unspeakable, unsocialized desires.

Hitchcock's film takes off from Highsmith and multiplies her doubles. In realizing a world of doubles that cut across supposed clear-cut differences, he "considerably undercuts a specific moral impulse that is supposed to inform the work" (Elsaesser 1999, 8). Elsaesser connects this doubling to Hitchcock's formal ingenuity, to his dandyism and Wildean aesthetics. This makes his films queer, to be sure; it makes such queerness a part of the everyday. Hitchcock's world does not carry the threat that Highsmith delivers where doubling would undo the social world. Or, to put this another way: despite the considerable fear and suspense that Hitchcock generates—despite, let's say, the horror that attends the murder of Miriam—there is always the possibility of playing it for laughs. Hitchcock offers comic relief that might relieve anyone of the fear that the ordinary world is in danger of collapsing. Or might not.

"On the verge of the film, [there are] two Patricia H's— Patricia Hitchcock, Hitchcock's daughter in her most extensive part … and Patricia Highsmith" (Dolar 1992, 39). McGilligan notes that "Pat [Hitchcock] reveled in the Hitchcockian sense of humor, and indeed shared it. While she was growing up, she has said, her father would sneak in and paint a scary face on her as she slept, giving her a start when she woke up and looked in the mirror. The father's daughter doubles the joke in a film full of mirrored meanings ... a constant reminder that behind the camera her father is chuckling" (2003, 453).

Patricia Hitchcock stands in for her chuckling father; she stands in for Highsmith, too, replaces her, playing her doubling game to another end. The character of Barbara, written for Patricia Hitchcock, is not in the novel; she's one of the film's many doubling additions. In herself, she (Barbara/Patricia) is not one. In the film, she doubles both Anne and Miriam; outside the film she doubles her father and the novelist. She is the wisecracking kid sister who says unspeakable things; her father in the film chastises her for saying what is on her (but really Hitchcock's) mind. Senator Morton's defense of Miriam—she was a human being—seems a futile gesture after Barbara dismisses her as a tramp and as an impediment to Guy and Anne. What she says is pretty much what Bruno said to Guy on the train. And then she becomes Miriam at her father's party. The voice of the anti-social, Barbara demonstrates how Hitchcock inhabits Highsmith's world and makes it his. She is certainly his queerest creation in the film.

REFERENCES

Allen, Richard. 2007. *Hitchcock's Romantic Irony*. New York: Columbia
   University Press.

Alpert, Hollis. 1951. "Some Hitchcock Murder & Some Pinza Marriage."
   Saturday Review 34 (July 14): 32.

Auiler, Dan. 1999. *Hitchcock's Notebooks*. New York: Avon.

Barrios, Richard. 2003. *Screened Out: Playing Gay in Hollywood from
   Edison to Stonewall*. New York: Routledge.

Barton, Sabrina. 1993. "'Crisscross': Paranoia and Projection in *Strangers on
   a Train*." In *Male Trouble*, edited by Constance Penley and Sharon Willis,
   (235–61). Minneapolis: University of Minnesota Press.

Benchley, Nathaniel. 1951. "Off Stage." *Theatre Arts* 35 (August): 28–29.

Bersani, Leo. 1995. *Homos*. Cambridge: Harvard University Press.

Carringer, Robert L. 2001. "Collaboration and Concepts of Authorship."
   PMLA 116 (2) (March): 370–79.

Clark, Jim. 2002. "Analysis of a Scene: *Strangers on a Train*." *Jim's Film
   Website* (July 25). http://jclarkmedia.com/film/filmanalysisstrangers.
   html.

Corber, Robert J. 1993. *In the Name of National Security: Hitchcock,
   Homophobia and the Political Construction of Gender in Postwar
   America*. Durham: Duke University Press.

Creekmur, Corey K. and Alexander Doty, eds. 1995. *Out in Culture: Gay,
   Lesbian, and Queer Essays on Popular Culture*. Durham: Duke University
   Press.

Crowther, Bosley. 1951a. "'Strangers on a Train,' Another Hitchcock
   Venture, Arrives at the Warner Theatre." *New York Times* (July 4):13.

———. 1951b. "Dexterity in a Void: Mr. Hitchcock Juggles in 'Strangers on a

Train.'" *New York Times*, section II (July 8):1.

"Current Feature Films." 1951. *The Christian Century* 68 (August 8): 927

Desowitz, Bill. 1992. "Life with Video: Strangers on Which Train?" *Film Comment* 28 (3): 4–5.

Dolar, Mladen. 1992. "Hitchcock's Objects"; "The Spectator Who Knew Too Much." In Žižek 1992, 31–46, 129–39.

Dyer, Richard. 1993. *The Matter of Images*. London: Routledge.

Edelman, Lee. 1999. "Rear Window's Glasshole." In *Out Takes: Essays on Queer Theory and Film*, edited by Ellis Hanson (72–96). Durham: Duke University Press.

———. 2004. *No Future: Queer Theory and the Death Drive*. Durham: Duke University Press.

Elsaesser, Thomas. 1999. "The Dandy in Hitchcock." In *Alfred Hitchcock: Centenary Essays*, edited by Richard Allen and S. Ishii-Gonzalès. London: British Film Institute, 3–13.

Farber, Manny. 1951. Films. *The Nation* (July 8): 77–78.

———. 2009. Clutter. In *Farber on Film*, edited by Robert Polito (602–15). New York: Library of America.

Gottlieb, Sidney, ed. 2003. *Alfred Hitchcock Interviews*. Jackson: University of Mississippi Press.

Granger, Farley. 2007. *Include Me Out*. New York: St. Martin's Griffin.

Hartung, Philip T. 1951. "Tennis Anyone?" *The Commonweal* 54:358–59.

Hatch, Kristen. 2005. 1951: "Movies and the New Faces of Masculinity." In *American Cinema of the 1950s*, edited by Murray Pomerance (43–64). New Brunswick, NJ: Rutgers University Press.

Hepworth, John. 1995. "Hitchcock's Homophobia." In Creekmur and Doty, 186–96.

Highsmith, Patricia. 2001. *Strangers on a Train*. New York: W.W. Norton & Co.

Kael, Pauline. 1991. *5001 Nights*. New York: Henry Holt & Co.

Krohn, Bill. 2000. *Hitchcock at Work*. New York: Phaidon.

LaValley, Albert J. 1972. *Focus on Hitchcock*. Englewood Cliffs, NJ: Prentice-Hall, Inc.

Lennon, Peter, 2001. "Surfer on the New Wave." *The Guardian* (June 16).

Lewes, Kenneth. 1995. *Psychoanalysis and Male Homosexuality*. Northvale, NJ: Jason Aronson Inc.

Linet, Beverly. 1986. *Star-Crossed: The Story of Robert Walker and Jennifer Jones*. New York: G.P. Putnam's Sons.

Luhr, William. 1982. *Raymond Chandler and Film*. New York: Frederick Ungar.

MacShane, Frank, ed. 1981. *Selected Letters of Raymond Chandler*. New York: Columbia University Press.

McGilligan, Patrick. 2003. *Alfred Hitchcock: A Life in Darkness and Light*. Chichester: Wiley.

Miller, D.A. 1990. "Anal *Rope*." *Representations* 32: 114–33.

———. 2010. "Hitchcock's Hidden Pictures." *Critical Inquiry* 37: 106–30.

Modleski, Tania. 2005. *The Women Who Knew Too Much: Hitchcock and Feminist Theory*. New York: Routledge.

Mogg, Ken. 2008. *The Alfred Hitchcock Story*. London: Titan.

Mulvey, Laura. 1975. "Visual Pleasure and Narrative Cinema." *Screen* 16(3): 6–18.

"Murder on the Merry-Go-Round." 1951. *Life* 31 no. 2 (July 9): 70–72.

Paglia, Camille. 1998. *The Birds*. London: British Film Institute.

Phillips, Gene D. 2000. *Creatures of Darkness: Raymond Chandler, Detective Fiction, and Film Noir*. Lexington: University Press of Kentucky.

Porter, Darwin. 2009. *Merv Griffin: A Life in the Closet*. [n.p.]: Blood Moon Productions Ltd.

Price, Theodore. 1992. *Hitchcock and Homosexuality: His 50-Year Obsession with Jack the Ripper and the Superbitch Prostitute—A Psychoanalytic View*. Metuchen, NJ: Scarecrow Press.

Rohmer, Eric and Claude Chabrol. 1979. *Hitchcock: The First Forty-Four Films*. Trans. Stanley Hochman. New York: Frederick Ungar.

Russo, Vito. 1987. *The Celluloid Closet*. New York: Harper & Row.

Schantz, Ned. 2008. *Gossip, Letters, Phones: The Scandal of Female Networks in Film and Literature*. Oxford: Oxford University Press.

———. 2010. "Hospitality and the Unsettled Viewer: Hitchcock's Shadow Scenes." *Camera Obscura* 73 (25.1): 1–26.

Schenkar, Joan. 2009. *The Talented Miss Highsmith: The Secret Life and Serious Art of Patricia Highsmith*. New York: St. Martin's Press.

Sedgwick, Eve Kosofsky. 1990. *Epistemology of the Closet*. Berkeley: University of California Press.

Spoto, Donald. 1976. *The Art of Alfred Hitchcock*. New York: Hopkinson and Blake.

———. 1983. *The Dark Side of Genius*. Boston: Little, Brown & Co.

Taylor, John Russell. 1978. *Hitch: The Life and Times of Alfred Hitchcock*. New York: Pantheon.

Toles, George. 2009. "The Forgotten Lighter and Other Moral Accidents in *Strangers on a Train*." *Raritan* 28(4): 111–37.

Truffaut, François. 1983. *Hitchcock*. New York: Simon & Schuster, Inc.

Tyler, Parker. 1973. *Screening the Sexes*. Garden City, NY: Doubleday.

Walker, Michael. 2005. *Hitchcock's Motifs*. Amsterdam: Amsterdam University Press.

Wood, Robin. 1995. "The Murderous Gays: Hitchcock's Homophobia." In Creekmur and Doty, 197–215.

———. 2002. *Hitchcock's Films Revisited*. New York: Columbia University Press.

Žižek, Slavoj. 1989. *The Sublime Object of Ideology*. London: Verso.

———. 1991. *Looking Awry: An Introduction to Jacques Lacan through Popular Culture*. Cambridge, MA: MIT Press.

———, ed. 1992. *Everything You Always Wanted to Know About Lacan ... But Were Afraid to Ask Hitchcock*. London: Verso.

FILMOGRAPHY

Der amerikanische freund (*The American Friend*). Wim Wenders. 1977.
Germany. 125 minutes.

The Birds. Alfred Hitchcock. 1963. USA. 119 minutes.

The Clock. Vincente Minnelli. 1945. USA. 90 minutes.

Murder! Alfred Hitchcock. 1930. UK. 104 minutes.

North by Northwest. Alfred Hitchcock. 1959. USA. 136 minutes.

One Touch of Venus. William Seiter. 1948. USA. 82 minutes.

Plein soleil (Purple Noon). René Clément. 1960. France. 118 minutes.

Psycho. Alfred Hitchcock. 1960. USA. 109 minutes.

Rear Window. Alfred Hitchcock. 1954. USA. 112 minutes.

Rebecca. Alfred Hitchcock. 1940. USA. 130 minutes.

Ripley's Game. Liliana Cavani. 2002. Italy. 110 minutes.

Rope. Alfred Hitchcock. 1948. USA. 80 minutes.

Side Street. Anthony Mann. 1950. USA. 83 minutes.

Stage Fright. Alfred Hitchcock. 1950. UK. 110 minutes.

Sunset Boulevard. Billy Wilder. 1950. USA. 110 minutes.

The Talented Mr. Ripley. Anthony Minghella. 1999. USA. 139 minutes.

They Live by Night. Nicholas Ray. 1949. USA. 95 minutes.

Le cri du hibou (The Cry of the Owl). Claude Chabrol. 1987. France. 102
minutes.

Vertigo. Alfred Hitchcock. 1958. USA. 128 minutes.

The Wrong Man. Alfred Hitchcock. 1956. USA. 105 minutes.

INDEX

Jonathan Goldberg is Arts and Sciences Distinguished
Professor of English at Emory University in Atlanta, where he
has directed the Studies in Sexualities Program since 2008. He
was previously Sir William Osler Professor of English at The
Johns Hopkins University, and also has held positions at Duke,
Brown, and Temple. He is the author of a number of books in
early modern studies, many of which focus on questions of
gender, sexuality, and materiality; they include *Writing Matter*,
Sodometries, *Desiring Women Writing*, *Tempest in the Caribbean*,
and *The Seeds of Things*. He is also the author of *Willa Cather
and Others*, and the editor of *Reclaiming Sodom* and *Queering
the Renaissance*. Most recently, he edited Eve Kosofsky
Sedgwick's posthumous 2012 book *The Weather in Proust*.

About the editors

MATTHEW HAYS is a Montreal-based critic, author, film festival programmer, and university instructor. His first book, *The View from Here: Conversations with Gay and Lesbian Filmmakers* (Arsenal Pulp Press), won a 2008 Lambda Literary Award. His articles have appeared numerous publications, including *The Guardian, The Daily Beast, The Globe and Mail, The New York Times, The Walrus, The Advocate, Maclean's, The Toronto Star, The International Herald Tribune, Cineaste, Cineaction, Quill & Quire, This Magazine, The Hollywood Reporter, Canadian Screenwriter, Xtra* and *fab*. He teaches courses in journalism, communication studies and film studies at Concordia University, where he received his MA in communication studies in 2000. A two-time nominee for a National Magazine Award, Hays received the 2007 Concordia Alumni Teaching Excellence Award.

THOMAS WAUGH is the award-winning author of numerous books, including five for Arsenal Pulp Press: *Out/Lines, Lust Unearthed, Gay Art: A Historic Collection* (with Felix Lance Falkon), *Comin' at Ya!* (with David Chapman), and *Montreal Main: A Queer Film Classic* (with Jason Garrison). His other books include *Hard to Imagine, The Fruit Machine,* and *The Romance of Transgression in Canada.* He teaches film studies at Concordia University in Montreal, Canada, where he lives. He has taught and published widely on political discourses and sexual representation in film and video, on queer film and video, and has developed interdisciplinary research and teaching on AIDS. He is also the founder and coordinator of the program in Interdisciplinary Studies in Sexuality at Concordia.